Garden Birds

Newman's Garden Birds

A householder's guide to the common birds
of the urban areas of South Africa
illustrated by the author

All photographs by the author unless otherwise stated

KENNETH NEWMAN

SOUTHERN
BOOK PUBLISHERS

In memory of Elisabeth

Copyright © 1991 by Kenneth Newman

All rights reserved. No part of this publication may be reproduced or transmitted in any form or by any means without prior written permission from the publisher.

ISBN 1 86812 335 9

First edition, first impression 1991
First edition, second impression 1992

Published by
Southern Book Publishers (Pty) Ltd
P O Box 3103, Halfway House 1685

Cover design by the author
Illustrations by the author
Set in 11 on 12 pt Andover
by Unifoto, Cape Town
Printed and bound by Creda Press (Pty) Ltd Cape Town

Contents

	PAGE
WHERE TO START	1
Introduction	2
Getting to know birds	4
Plumage	5
Display	6
Territories	8
Distribution and habitats	8
Feet and bills	10
What birds eat	10
Nests and nest-building	11
Attracting birds to the garden	12
Feeding	12
Water	14
Planting for birds	14
Nest-sites	14
The use of poisons in the garden	15
Caring for young birds	17
Casualties among adult birds	19
How to use this book	**20**
Basic key-map	21
Birds' eggs	22
A warning	22
DESCRIPTIONS OF BIRDS	23

Common name	Scientific name	Page
Hamerkop	*Scopus umbretta*	24
Hadeda Ibis	*Bostrychia hagedash*	26
Rock Pigeon	*Columba guinea*	28
Cape Turtle Dove	*Streptopelia capicola*	30
Redeyed Dove	*Streptopelia semitorquata*	30
Laughing Dove	*Streptopelia senegalensis*	32
Grey Lourie	*Corythaixoides concolor*	34
Redchested Cuckoo	*Cuculus solitarius*	36
Diederik Cuckoo	*Chrysococcyx caprius*	38
Burchell's Coucal	*Centropus superciliosus*	40
Barn Owl	*Tyto alba*	42
Spotted Eagle Owl	*Bubo africanus*	44
Greater Striped Swallow	*Hirundo cucullata*	46
Lesser Striped Swallow	*Hirundo abyssinica*	46
Whiterumped Swift	*Apus caffer*	48
Little Swift	*Apus affinis*	48
Whitebacked Mousebird	*Colius colius*	50
Speckled Mousebird	*Colius striatus*	50
Redfaced Mousebird	*Colius indicus*	52
Giant Kingfisher	*Ceryle maxima*	54
Malachite Kingfisher	*Alcedo cristata*	56
Hoopoe	*Upupa epops*	58
Redbilled Woodhoopoe	*Phoeniculus purpureus*	60

Blackcollared Barbet	*Lybius torquatus*	62
Crested Barbet	*Trachyphonus vailantii*	64
Cape Wagtail	*Motacilla capensis*	66
Pied Crow	*Corvus albus*	68
Blackeyed Bulbul	*Pycnonotus barbatus*	70
Cape Bulbul	*Pycnonotus capensis*	70
Kurrichane Thrush	*Turdus libonyana*	72
Olive Thrush	*Turdus olivaceus*	72
Natal Robin	*Cossypha natalensis*	74
Cape Robin	*Cossypha caffra*	76
Garden Warbler	*Sylvia borin*	78
European Marsh Warbler	*Acrocephalus palustris*	78
Willow Warbler	*Phylloscopus trochilus*	78
Tawnyflanked Prinia	*Prinia subflava*	80
Blackchested Prinia	*Prinia flavicans*	80
Fiscal Flycatcher	*Sigelus silens*	82
Paradise Flycatcher	*Terpsiphone viridis*	84
Fiscal Shrike	*Lanius collaris*	86
Southern Boubou	*Laniarius ferrugineus*	88
Puffback	*Dryoscopus cubla*	90
Bokmakierie	*Telophorus zeylonus*	92
European Starling	*Sturnus vulgaris*	94
Indian Myna	*Acridotheres tristis*	94
Plumcoloured Starling	*Cinnyricinclus leucogaster*	96
Cape Glossy Starling	*Lamprotornis nitens*	98
Redwinged Starling	*Onychognathus morio*	100
Malachite Sunbird	*Nectarinia famosa*	102
Black Sunbird	*Nectarinia amethystina*	102
Lesser Doublecollared Sunbird	*Nectarinia chalybea*	104
Greater Doublecollared Sunbird	*Nectarinia afra*	104
Whitebellied Sunbird	*Nectarinia talatala*	106
Cape White-eye	*Zosterops pallidus*	108
House Sparrow	*Passer domesticus*	110
Cape Sparrow	*Passer melanurus*	110
Spectacled Weaver	*Ploceus ocularis*	112
Spottedbacked Weaver	*Ploceus cucullatus*	112
Cape Weaver	*Ploceus capensis*	114
Masked Weaver	*Ploceus velatus*	116
Red Bishop	*Euplectes orix*	118
Bronze Mannikin	*Spermestes cucullatus*	120
Pintailed Whydah	*Vidua macroura*	122
Cape Canary	*Serinus canicollis*	124
Yelloweyed Canary	*Serinus mozambicus*	124

Appendix 126

References 127

Where to Start

Introduction

Since this book was first published in 1967 bird-watching has undergone a tremendous transition. From being the hobby of a comparative few it has mushroomed into the pursuit of millions throughout the western world, and new adherents throng to join their ranks. The origins of this great interest can probably be found in a new awareness and appreciation of all wild things engendered by numerous television programmes by world leaders in the field of natural history. They have emphasised the need to conserve our natural heritage in the face of rapidly increasing human pressures. Familiarity with an animal, whether it be insect or whale, brings about an understanding of its ways, an appreciation of its requirements and an awareness of its place in the great mosaic of inter-relationships. Humankind is at last beginning to realise that all life has a place on this earth, and is taking a new look at the wild things around us. The fact that birds are high on this list is not surprising when one realises that in comparison to the many wild animals that can only be seen naturally in game reserves, birds are with us all the time.

South Africa has a rich and varied birdlife, over 800 species visiting or being resident within our borders in any year. Naturally, there is no part of the country in which all these species occur together. Some are forest residents, others prefer woodland, mountains, water or grassveld. Probably the greatest variety is to be found in the bushveld, but even in the Kruger National Park the number of recorded species is only a little more than half the country's total.

It is in one's own garden that one can get to know birds with the minimum of effort, simply by making the garden attractive to them. Some may feel that their garden is already too attractive to them, especially when the summer season's fruit is ripening, but with a little extra knowledge and understanding of their ways, even the home fruit grower will come to realise that birds are our allies rather than enemies.

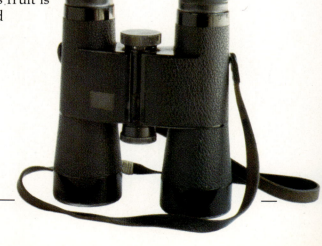

Helping the reader to get to know and understand birds is the prime purpose of this book. It is a householder's guide to garden bird-watching. In this revision some 20 new bird species have been added, bringing the total number to 64 species that qualify for the term 'garden birds', in itself an example of the dynamic nature of our avifauna. Perhaps more than any other animals birds are quick to take advantage of the new habitats provided over the years by the afforestation of urban areas in regions that had hitherto been devoid of the cover and breeding opportunities provided by shrubs and trees. While urban development deprives some birds of their habitats (grassland birds are the first to suffer in such cases) many others move in once the new settlement has 'mellowed'. Among the more notable new arrivals in many regions are the Hadeda Ibis, Grey Lourie, Puffback, Giant Kingfisher, swallows and swifts, all of which are now included in this book.

The novice bird-watcher is understandably daunted by the huge array of species presented by most South African bird books, not realising that the majority of birds illustrated in them have little chance of appearing in the average garden. Even when this fact is appreciated the task of finding and identifying that 'little yellow bird' in the garden is enormous because among our 800 or more there are many little yellow birds.

In *Newman's Garden Birds* all unlikely birds have been eliminated. Only those that one can expect to see in the average suburban garden of half a hectare or less are shown. In most gardens this will amount to no more than about 35 different birds during any day of the year, depending upon where one lives. Should the reader wish, in due course, to progress beyond this stage this book may be regarded as a stepping-stone to the more ambitious works, and it will have served to introduce yet another enthusiast to the colourful and fascinating world of South African birds.

Getting to know birds

The study of birds is a science that occupies the attention of a host of workers, professional and amateur, in many countries. As a result of this research our knowledge of birds is being continually supplemented and our interpretations of their activities are subject to constant revision. The physiology of birds and their numerous patterns of behaviour are beset with so many complexities, exceptions and difficulties of interpretation that it would take several pages to offer even a simplified account of any one of them. Therefore this introductory chapter will be limited to giving the budding bird-watcher an outline of a bird's physical make-up, with some information about the types of birds to be seen, and a guide to their behaviour. This will also familiarise the reader with the various ornithological terms used in this book.

Though birds differ in size, shape and general behaviour, when they are considered in relation to other animals it will be seen that they are comparatively uniform. Mammals and insects, for instance, may be shaped for a life of walking, swimming, wriggling or burrowing, whereas birds are primarily designed for one thing: flight. Their entire structure, in every detail, is a perfect example of the way in which natural selection has answered the stringent specifications imposed by flight. The result is a sound aerodynamic design, unequalled by man-made aircraft.

The bone structure of a bird is extremely light though rigid, being little more than a series of plates and struts. Many of the bones are hollow and, in some of the larger birds, internally stiffened with a series of cross-braced reinforcements, not unlike the skeleton of an airship. Anyone who has examined the carcass of a chicken will be aware of the greatly enlarged and keeled breastbone which is common to all flying birds and which carries the wing muscles, the strongest and heaviest muscles in the body. Flightless birds, such as the Ostrich, lack this keeled breastbone.

In relative size a bird's brain is about equal to that of a very small mammal. Those parts of the brain concerned with co-ordination of movement and instinctive memory are comparatively larger, whereas that part concerned with learning is smaller. The brain is set at the back of the head while the eyes, which are enormous in proportion to the skull, occupy a very large area in front of the brain. A bird's eyes are among the most highly developed in the animal kingdom, and in the larger birds of prey are larger than human eyes.

The flesh covering of a wild, free-flying bird is trimmed to the minimum necessary to cover the skeletal framework. The excess fat seen on domestic birds bred for the table is usually the result of special or forced feeding and limited exercise, and is unlikely to be seen in a wild bird. On the other hand wild birds do store some fat under their skins for purposes of insulation. Sometimes, prior to migration and before winter in temperate climates, this fat is built up in quite large quantities to provide an extra food supply.

Feathers are a unique characteristic of birds and, both as a body covering and as an implement of flight, are extremely efficient. They provide the bird with an ultra-light protective covering which is both a good thermal insulator and a streamlined surface for motion, whether this be in the air, on the ground or in water.

An adult bird has feathers of several types, the majority of those visible being called 'contour' feathers. These are the primaries on the outer wing, the secondaries on the inner wing or forearm, the tail feathers and those that form the outer covering on the body. Beneath these in many places are the down feathers, which are usually smaller and softer than the contour feathers and provide the bird with a warm undercoat.

Other types of feathers are the delicate unbarbed 'filoplumes' that grow on certain parts of a bird's body and are usually concealed but are visible in some cases; the stiff bristle-like feathers that grow near the base of the bill or as eyelashes; and the large ornamental ones that some birds grow from their tails, heads or other parts of the body. These are usually modified contour feathers and may be discarded and regrown at regular intervals.

Birds have very large eyes in proportion to the size of their heads, and extremely acute vision. This is the eye of a Secretarybird. Photo: Peter Steyn.

Plumage

It is extremely important that a bird's plumage be kept in good condition if it is to function efficiently in flight, as an insulator and as a waterproof covering. Feather maintenance activities therefore have an important place in a bird's daily life, and much time is devoted to them. These activities include bathing in fresh water and grooming the feathers with the bill, or 'preening'. When a bird preens it cleans and rearranges its feathers by stroking them with its bill and by running them individually through the partly opened bill. These actions are frequently associated with 'oiling': the anointing of the plumage with oil from the special preen-gland above the root of the tail.

A major contribution to feather maintenance is the periodical moult, which occurs annually in some birds and twice or even three times a year in others. The moult consists of the shedding and renewal of feathers, and is usually connected with the breeding season, or with migration in those birds that migrate.

In most birds the moult occurs gradually so that their powers of flight are unimpeded, but others, notably certain members of the duck family, moult all their primary feathers simultaneously and thus are rendered flightless for a period. At this time these ducks retire to large, open expanses of water until they are able to fly again.

A young bird generally acquires full adult plumage towards the end of the first year, but in some of the larger species it may take several years, the immature bird progressing through several forms of intermediate plumage. Many young birds resemble the adult female in coloration, while some have a distinctive plumage colouring quite different from either parent.

Both the newly hatched Crowned Plover and the unhatched egg are cryptically coloured to match the surroundings.

The young of many terrestrial birds, such as plovers and bustards, are coloured with disruptive or outline-breaking patterns which cause them to blend with their surroundings. Such young instinctively flatten themselves on the ground, remaining motionless when danger threatens, and are very difficult to see even when their presence is known. Yet other birds, like partridges and snipes, retain this cryptic coloration all their lives.

Bright colours and conspicuous markings may have numerous and diverse functions, but it is thought that they are important as a means of communication between members of a pair in a large group, in distinguishing between the bird's own species and others, and in display.

Brightly coloured plumage is frequently present in the male of a species only, the female being a drab colour which renders it less conspicuous when sitting on the nest or carrying food to the young, and this may be a form of protection. In moments of danger the brightly coloured cock often displays itself prominently, an innate action that may cause predators to be distracted from the hen and nest. On the other hand birds that nest in cavities are often brightly coloured in both sexes, good examples being the barbets.

This Threebanded Courser is almost invisible against the background of dry grass.

Display

Display can best be defined as signalling, and can take the form of body movements, postures, plumage rearrangements, calls and other more subtle actions. The type of distraction display that is common in birds with bright colours has already been mentioned, but there are other forms that do not use colour as the main distractor. Many of the ground-nesting birds, for instance, will simulate injury by limping along the ground with their wings trailing as though wounded, but always away

This Lesser Striped Swallow preening its shoulder feathers.

from the nest or young, to encourage the suspected predator to follow them in that direction in the expectation of an easy kill. Other forms of display are threat, submission, courtship, greeting and anti-predator.

Threat display is likely to be seen among garden birds when several individuals are at the bird table. The usual signs of aggression involve the head being held forward with the body horizontal and directed towards the opponent, or the head held high with the bill pointing skywards and the breast directed towards the rival. In response to this the rival may adopt a submissive attitude, crouching slightly with the head withdrawn and the feathers raised, or it may merely move off or respond with a display of counter-aggression. In the last case the feathers may fly and this often happens when the opponents are sparrows.

A Crowned Plover spreads its wings in display, revealing the bold colours of the under-surface. Such displays, accompanied by loud vocalisation, are used to distract would-be predators away from the ground-nest.

The anti-predator display is also likely to be seen in the garden sooner or later. This is frequently caused by a cat or snake, but is also directed at predatory birds. The display involves a number of birds of different species, all of which gather around the predator at a safe distance and call or chatter incessantly, the resulting clamour attracting more and more birds to the scene. Often the noise itself is instrumental in causing the predator to leave, but in certain circumstances bolder individuals among the birds may even press home a physical attack on the bewildered would-be aggressor.

Courtship display has an important part in the lives of most birds, the male bird playing the more active role in some cases, while both sexes participate actively in others. Courtship displays are many and varied and may involve the spreading of wings or tail, or both; erecting the feathers on the nape or on the back; special display flights and many other rituals. Perhaps one of the best known is that of the peacock, which fans its tail feathers while approaching the hen, while the most advanced and complicated forms of display are those performed by members of the bird of paradise family in New Guinea. Many males in this group are adorned with extremely ornate plumes which they wave, dangle or shake within sight of the opposite sex.

The well-known display of the male Peacock in which the tail feathers are raised and spread. Photo: Vernon Alder.

In a crowded colony such as is seen in the Cape Gannet and many other seabirds the breeding territory of a pair is determined by the pecking range of the sitting bird's beak.

Territories

When an area is defended by a bird, or pair of birds, against others of the same species it is called a territory. Territories are formed to defend an exclusive feeding region, for mating or to effect the spacing of pairs. Territories of various sizes are established and are held for varying lengths of time. An eagle, for instance, may have a territory with boundaries many kilometres apart, while a colonial bird, nesting as a member of a compact group, may hold a territory the span of which is defined by the reach of the bird's bill while it is sitting on the nest. Similarly territories vary with garden birds. In colonial-nesting weavers the territory of a pair may be a tree or even part of a tree, while that of a pair of robins may extend to a whole garden or several gardens.

Many migratory birds establish a territory for the duration of their sojourn in a particular locality, and may or may not re-establish it in the same place the following season, while many sedentary birds hold a territory for life.

Establishing a territory does not guarantee freedom from intrusion, and thus a considerable part of a male bird's time is spent in defending its domain from other males of the same species. This involves threat display or, if necessary, direct attack on the trespasser. Territorial defence is usually the role of the male bird among garden species, and the male's appearance on the scene is often sufficient to cause the withdrawal of the intruder.

Distribution and habitats

One of the first things that may strike the user of this book is the uneven distribution of some birds. Species that are common in one region are uncommon in or entirely absent from another. These limitations are often associated with specific food or habitat requirements or climatic conditions. Thus the Natal Robin, being a denizen of evergreen forests, is confined to those areas in Natal and further north where such conditions still exist. Many other species that are not garden birds have similar strong habitat preferences. Some are dependent on fynbos where *proteas, ericas* and other such plants provide them with the nectar they need to feed on, and even the plant down needed for their nests. Others again are adapted to a life in the grassveld: larks and some pipits fall into this category.

Climatic conditions also play a part in determining the spread of birds. It will be seen from the distribution maps that many garden birds are entirely absent from the drier parts of the country. Others may temporarily appear in these regions during seasons of high rainfall.

But the ranges of some birds are limited for reasons that are not clear. Why, for instance, is the Cape Bulbul confined to a broad coastal strip between the Orange River mouth and Port Elizabeth, whereas the Blackeyed Bulbul, with apparently similar feeding and habitat requirements, is common elsewhere but not in that region? The distributions of the Crested and Blackcollared Barbets are also puzzling in that neither occurs in the western Cape although, being a fruit-growing district, it would appear to offer every attraction to these frugivorous birds.

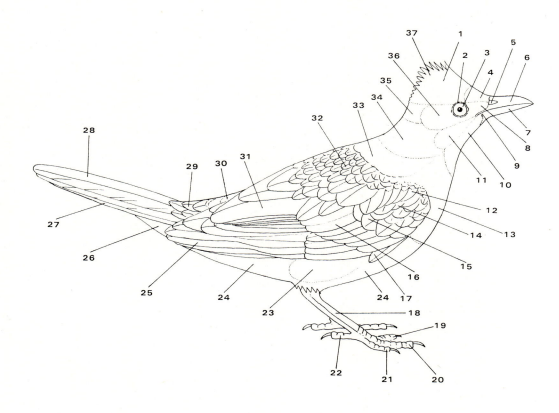

DIAGRAM OF THE PARTS OF A BIRD

1 Crown	11 Cheek	21 Fourth toe	30 Rump
2 Eyelid	12 Shoulder	22 First toe	31 Secondaries
3 Iris	13 Breast	23 Flank	32 Scapulars
4 Forehead	14 Lesser wing-coverts	24 Abdomen	33 Mantle
5 Nostril	15 Median wing-coverts	25 Primaries	34 Neck
6 Upper mandible	16 Primary wing-coverts	26 Under tail-coverts (or vent)	35 Nape
7 Lower mandible	17 Alula (bastard wing)	27 Outer tail-feathers	36 Ear-coverts
8 Lores	18 Tarsus	28 Central tail-feather	37 Crest
9 Gape	19 Second toe	29 Upper tail-coverts	
10 Throat	20 Third toe		

Feet and bills

The feet and bill of a bird are usually adapted to its way of feeding. Obvious examples of this are the long legs of birds that wade in water (herons, flamingoes and some plovers) or walk in long grass (storks, bustards, the Secretarybird and others), and the webbed feet of swimming birds. We also see a clear example in the enormous feet of the jacanas, or lily-trotters, the elongated toes of which distribute their mass over a large area and enable them to walk on water lily leaves.

Most of our garden birds have four fairly equal toes suited to perching, three in front and one at the back of the foot. Birds with these feet belong to a very large group called the passerines. Variations to this foot structure can be seen in the cuckoos, coucals, barbets, woodpeckers, mousebirds and some others, in which the outer toe is reversible so that it may be turned to either the front or back of the foot. Such birds are said to have zygodactylus feet which often, in association with short legs, are an adaptation to climbing.

Birds' bills vary to a marked degree and are usually adapted to their type of food or method of obtaining it. Here again, obvious examples are the very long bills of water- or mud-probing birds as seen in the herons, ibis and snipe or the spacious fish-carrying bills of pelicans.

We see some interesting examples of specialised bills among the garden birds. The long curved bill of the Hoopoe is used for probing the ground, while the slender curved bills of the sunbirds enable them to reach deep into flowers to extract nectar.

Birds that eat only soft-bodied insects usually have bills of slender proportions, examples being the Paradise Flycatcher, migrant warblers and prinias. Compare these with the stout, hooked bill of the Fiscal Shrike which is suited to a more carnivorous diet.

Seed-eaters have strong, short bills to crack hard seeds and seed-pods. Typical of this group are the sparrows, weavers and canaries.

What birds eat

The normal or preferred diets of the birds dealt with in this book are given in the description of each species, but one cannot be dogmatic about it. Most birds eat a variety of foods, with certain things being favoured when they are available. It would be wrong, for example, to describe the Laughing Dove as insectivorous, but it will eat large quantities of flying termites when these insects are swarming, as do many other species: bulbuls, robins, shrikes, starlings, sparrows and weavers, to name but a few.

The feeding patterns of birds often change with the seasons, so that in summer when fruit is plentiful birds like the Masked Weaver, which usually eats seeds and insects, will gorge on figs to the exclusion of everything else while the supply lasts. Again, many that normally eat seeds feed their nestlings with insects, probably an instinctive recognition of the fact that growing young need protein.

Nests and nest-building

The types of nests built by birds, and the materials used, are as varied as the birds themselves. Nest types are often common to a family or group of birds, most species within that group following a similar pattern, such as woodpeckers and barbets excavating trees or doves and pigeons constructing a simple platform of twigs.

In many species the female is responsible for selecting the nest site, but in other cases, notably the weavers, the male makes the initial choice. In some species, too, both sexes gather material and build, while in others this is done by one sex only. Perhaps the most fascinating aspect of nest-building is the way in which each bird instinctively builds to the correct design, even though it may be nesting for the first time. Even a young bird, removed from its nest before its eyes are open, and hand-reared to maturity without contact with its own kind, given the opportunity to breed naturally, will build a nest identical to that in which it was born.

Another thing that seldom fails to impress us is the industry that some birds put into nest construction. This may entail the finding and carrying of over a thousand pieces of material before the nest is finished. In contrast to this are the 'nests' of many terrestrial birds that make do with a simple scrape.

Birds nesting near human habitations are likely to make use of discarded household materials for their nests. Birds also take advantage of the domestic scene in other ways. Robins and wagtails will nest in flower pots, watering cans and garden sheds, while House Sparrows, for example, prefer a cavity in a house to one in a tree. Many birds nest in close juxtaposition to human dwellings by choice, perhaps considering these sites to be relatively safe from predators. This phenomenon is particularly noticeable in the vicinity of country hotels, game lodges and farm houses.

RIGHT *This Black Flycatcher has chosen to place its nest in the top of a ventilation pipe.*

LEFT *This nest of a pair of Kurrichane Thrushes is placed in the gutter of a house. Photo: Peter Steyn.*

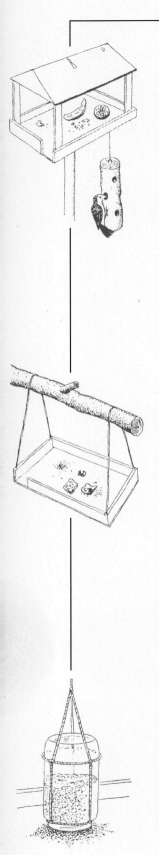

Attracting birds to the garden

There are several ways to encourage birds into your garden. You may feed them, provide water and create conditions suitable for nesting. But before doing any of these things, take steps to ensure that they can come in safety. If cats frequent the garden there will be a tragedy unless you do something to prevent it.

The surest way of barring unwanted cat visitors is to enclose your grounds with a wire mesh fence. This need not look unsightly if a creeper or quick-growing hedge is planted next to it. Another method is to cultivate a dense or prickly hedge, but you will still need to block gaps close to the ground. In any case, if you intend to feed birds be sure to put the food away from any low cover from which cats can pounce. In this regard the safest way is to erect a bird table as detailed below. If you own a cat it is a good idea to feed the birds at a regular time each day, say early mornings, and to confine the cat during that period. The birds will soon learn at what time meals are served.

Feeding

There is a body of opinion that frowns on feeding birds regularly, on the premise that they will come to rely on it and suffer in consequence should circumstances prevent one's continuing to feed them. This may well apply in the harsh winter conditions found in European countries, but in South Africa even in mid-winter our climate is never so harsh that birds would be without an alternative food source. Should you have fears in this respect, a moderate offering of food at a fixed time daily will certainly not encourage birds to become too dependent on your generosity.

The best way of feeding birds is to erect a special table for the purpose. This should be a flat piece of wood surmounting a pole or hanging from a branch, ideally within viewing distance of your window. The table itself can be an old kitchen tray or the base of a wooden box. If a pole mounting is used the pole should be smooth, a metal pole being the best. This will prevent cats, squirrels and rats from attempting to climb it. For the same reason, the table top should extend beyond the pole by about 300 mm all round.

A hanging table is an effective safeguard against cats but is no obstacle to squirrels or rats. So if there is any likelihood of these animals being present rather use the pole-mounted table. A skirting all round the table will prevent food from falling off (leave a small gap for brushing off stale food), and a roof is useful, though not essential, for protecting the food from sun and rain, and for suspending various feeders which are discussed below.

Birds can be attracted by a variety of foods, some being favoured by specific species. Bread, preferably wholemeal, in the form of crusts and

Laughing Doves feeding a pole-mounted bird table

stale loaves should be first moistened with water. An unbroken piece of bread will stay moist and edible longer than small pieces.

To encourage barbets, bulbuls, starlings, white-eyes and mousebirds, all sorts of blemished fruit can be bought from the greengrocer for a few cents, and will supplement the household rejects. Apples, pears, pawpaws, grapes, guavas, oranges and bananas seem to be preferred in that order, but take steps to ensure that the barbets cannot fly off with the food. These birds can pick up quite large pieces of apple and small bunches of grapes, so nail them to the table or put a piece of wire mesh over the fruit so that the birds are obliged to peck through it.

These half apples have been threaded onto large nails protruding from the base of the bird table. This prevents their being knocked to the ground or carried away by the larger birds.

For the seed-eaters wild bird seed is a favourite, but a cheaper buy is crushed maize which can be purchased from supermarkets. Other favourites are watermelon seeds and sunflower seeds. These can be put in a dish or loose on the table, but there is every likelihood that they will get scattered by the wind or by squabbling sparrows. A better way is to put the seeds in a hopper made from a glass jar suspended from the roof of the bird table and with the mouth just half a centimetre above the feeding surface. This will prevent any bird from monopolising the supply and will also protect the seed from rain.

Insectivorous birds are generally regarded as being difficult to attract to the bird table. Collecting insects from the garden is a tedious and time-consuming business, and can be done more efficiently by the birds themselves. Mealworms can be bought from some pet shops but they are rather expensive, are not always available and are usually eaten by the sparrows anyway. The answer is butcher's bone-meal, a mixture of finely ground meat and bone, often bought for dogs. Do not buy packeted bone-meal in powder form. Butcher's bone-meal is very cheap, a few cents' worth being sufficient to keep a bird table supplied for a week, and is irresistible to almost every kind of bird, whatever their normal diet. A handful should be put out daily to keep the supply fresh and fly-free.

Other important foods for birds are mealie pap and dog food. When scraping out the residue from the mealie pot — and there is invariably a lot stuck around the bottom — be sure to put it on the bird tray. Epol brand dog food, the granular type that needs to be mixed with water to make a stiff porridge, is irresistible to many birds. In fact both mealie pap and Epol dog food are relished by thrushes, barbets, bulbuls, doves, woodhoopoes, starlings, weavers and sparrows. Other foods that may be offered to birds are stale fruit cakes, bacon rind (cooked or raw), cheese rinds and, in winter, suet.

Water

Many birds obtain sufficient moisture from their food or from rain and dew droplets but others, especially doves and pigeons, must drink regularly to assist their digestive processes. Birds also like to bathe as part of their routine feather care.

A water feature can serve as an alternative or supplementary attraction to the bird table in your garden. An ornamental fish pond is one way of supplying this water. A shallow area should be created by submerging a large, flat stone near the centre of the pond away from cats. The stone should be about 20 mm below the surface, with a section of it above the water, or with another stone on it for the birds to settle on. Trickling water over rocks is also a great attraction. An elevated bird-bath, of the type sold by plant nurseries and hardware shops, is cat-proof. These are usually made of asbestos or concrete, but they should have a gently sloping depression with a rough finish to give the birds a foothold. If the centre of the bath is more than 50 mm below water when filled, some flat stones should be placed in it for the birds to stand on.

Planting for birds

Well-foliaged trees and bushes are a sure way of attracting birds to your garden. They provide good cover for roosting and nesting as well as ensuring a supply of insects. Areas of dense bush, especially evergreens, will be particularly appreciated by the ground-haunting robins, thrushes, Boubou Shrikes and Bokmakieries while ivy, honeysuckle and similar wall creepers may be used for nesting by many. The berries of variegated ivy are relished by bulbuls while honeysuckle flowers provide nectar for sunbirds and white-eyes. By far the best combination is to plant bushes and shrubs that provide food in the form of fruit, berries or nectar, as well as giving shelter. The list of suitable food plants is long, but some of the more popular indigenous ones are listed in the Appendix. This list should be consulted in collaboration with your nurseryman, who will advise on which are best suited to your area.

Nest-sites

Quite apart from the natural nesting places provided by bushes and trees, many birds can be encouraged to nest in the garden by the provision of nest-boxes or nest-logs. These, if suitable, will be used by the hole-nesting barbets, starlings, Mynas, Hoopoes and others. Nest-boxes should be well constructed and proofed against the weather. Leaking cracks or draughty gaps, which often appear after a season's exposure, will not be tolerated and must be filled or covered with waterproof material. The box should be firmly suspended on a post or tree at a height of at least two metres above ground, should face away from the sun and wind and should be clear of leafy branches. The

dimensions of the nest-box will depend largely on the type of bird you wish to attract. Blackcollared Barbets and sparrows will need internal measurements of not more than 80 mm square and 250 mm deep, with an entrance hole of no more than 40 mm diameter. Crested Barbets, Glossy Starlings and Redbilled Woodhoopoes will want a box with inner dimensions of about 100 mm × 100 mm, a depth of about 400 mm and an entrance hole of 60 mm diameter.

The most natural looking and successful type of nesting accommodation for birds is the nest-log. This can be a piece of willow branch of about a metre in length and with a diameter of 130 mm for smaller birds or 200 mm for larger birds. The log should be firmly wired to a tree or post, the positioning exactly as detailed for a nest-box. It is important that the log be fixed in such a way that it cannot slip or wobble. Should the tree be a fast-growing one, check occasionally that its expanding girth is not causing the wire to crush the log. It is not necessary to make a hole in the log if there are barbets or woodpeckers on hand, since they will prefer to make their own excavation. If there are no wood-boring birds in the vicinity then a piece of hollow bamboo or sisal is best used, to similar dimensions as given above. The entrance hole should follow the dimensions given for a nest-box, and should be made about 150 mm from the top. In the Witwatersrand region ready-made hardwood nest-logs may be purchased from certain nurseries and hardware shops.

In both boxes and logs sitting birds have the habit of pecking at the surrounding walls and base of the nest chamber (perhaps to provide a soft floor of wood chips?), and may well peck right through. This has to be watched for between seasons and repaired, along with other cracks, using wood-filler or a bituminised covering.

At this point a word of warning is necessary. Nesting birds are very sensitive to disturbance, especially during the stages of nest-building, egg-laying and early incubation. A strong nest-bond does not develop in a bird until incubation is well under way, and any interference before this is likely to cause desertion. Frequent or obvious visits to the nest should be avoided as predators are likely to follow your example (and your scent) with fatal results for the eggs or nestlings. It is safer by far to leave nesting birds alone and to observe them from a distance through binoculars. On no account look into the nest while the parent is sitting; there is probably nothing quite so frightening to a bird as a huge human face peering in and blocking its only exit.

The use of poisons in the garden

Many garden chemicals designed to kill insect pests are also potential killers of other living things, and the most dangerous ones, by far, are the persistent organo-chlorine insecticides. Although their initial toxicity may be low, they do not break down in nature but accumulate in the environment and may build up to dangerous levels. Tests have shown that these chemicals remain active for many years.

DDT was the first to be discovered and has therefore been in use for a long time. It is significant that, although it is one of the least harmful of the organo-chlorines, DDT residues have been found in living creatures all over the world; in wild birds in the USA and Europe; in fish in the rivers of the USA and Britain; in mammals in northern Canada; in sharks and other fishes in the Pacific Ocean; and in penguins and seals in the Antarctic. Even more frightening is the fact that it has been found in the food we eat and in our bodies. It therefore follows that if you use any of these persistent chemicals in your garden you are guilty of adding to world pollution.

These chemicals, when applied to gardens or crops, are washed into the soil by rain and subsequently contaminate our rivers. From there it is only a matter of time before they enter the sea, where there is no limit to the extent of their travels. Animals of all kinds collect these chemicals in their systems because they are in every food chain and cannot be eliminated. Their long-term effect on birds can be disastrous.

Birds that eat a number of contaminated insects obtain a large dose of the poison and are unable to eliminate it immediately, storing it in their fat reserves. The result, if not death to the bird when its fat reserves are called upon, is sometimes sterility. Eggs fail to hatch, or the shells are so thin that they break, or young do not reach maturity. In Europe and the USA certain birds of prey almost became extinct as a consequence of eating rodents that had been contaminated, in turn, by feeding on vegetables treated with these toxic chemicals.

It is the clear duty of everyone to safeguard not only their own health and that of their family, but of all living things, by refraining from using persistent organo-chlorine insecticides. Many of these poisons are still obtainable in the shops, and since their contents are not always apparent from their name, the small print must be read. The ones to be avoided are those containing aldrin, dieldrin, endrin, endosulfan, rhothane, DDT, BHC, lindane and chlordane.

The organo-phosphorous group includes some of the most toxic insect-killers known, such as malathion, and should also be used with the greatest care. Though this group has only limited persistence their immediate effects can be quite spectacular, and extremely dangerous to animals and human beings. Birds feeding on plants recently sprayed with malathion are likely to die within a very short time, and it is therefore most important that these insecticides be used in the minimum amounts specified on the product labels; are not used in windy weather; are preferably applied late in the evening when most birds and bees have ceased feeding; and that the user's hands and all implements be thoroughly washed immediately after use.

A SAFE GARDEN SPRAY

A really safe garden spray against aphids on flowers, vegetables and fruit can be easily made at home by adding to 20 litres of tepid water: one heaped tablespoon of bicarbonate of soda, two tablespoons of Jeyes Fluid and one-fifth of a bar of blue mottled soap (it must be blue mottled soap). The soap should be flaked and thoroughly mixed into the solution.

Other chemicals that appear to be reasonably safe in the long term and to warm-blooded creatures are those containing pyrethrum, derris and nicotine. Although these do not accumulate or have spectacular immediate results they are all poisons, and the instructions for their handling should be followed carefully.

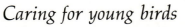

Caring for young birds

The soundest advice under this heading is: *Do not attempt it.* The majority of young birds are 'found' — before they are lost — by children or well-meaning adults with little or no understanding of a bird's needs. Usually the poor, forcibly adopted chick is put in a shoe-box, smothered in cotton-wool and slowly put to death on a diet of bread and milk.

It must be remembered that many young birds leave their nests in what appears to be a premature state of development, whereas in fact their care and feeding are continued by the parents long after they have left the nest. If a fledgeling is found out of the nest in what seems to be a dangerous situation the best procedure is to place it in some high but safe place where the parents can continue to give it their attention. If the young bird initially refuses to remain where you have placed it cover it temporarily with a hat or piece of cloth; the darkness will calm it. *On no account should it be taken more than a few metres from where it was first found.* Once relaxed and left alone the chick will commence calling and the parents will locate it.

If the bird is a nestling, that is to say a young bird without proper feather development on its wings, or unable to stand on its feet for any length of time, it should, if possible, be replaced in the nest. Before doing this check that the nest is not infested with ants. Only when replacement in the nest is clearly impossible, or when the parents are known to have deserted or been killed, should an attempt be made to rear the young bird, because the task is formidable.

First establish the identity of the bird in order to determine its diet. Should it be the chick of a seed-eater it is fairly safe to assume that it will thrive on an insect diet in the early stages, but there are exceptions to this rule. Birds that normally eat insects in their adult life can also be given the same diet from the start, but many of the fruit-eaters feed their young on soft fruit and specific insects only, such as termites.

Most young birds of the species described in this book will need feeding about every half hour of the daylight hours, and this can involve several 'mouthfuls' each time. The need for more food can usually be judged by the persistence with which the youngster begs for more with bill wide open. If the chick is being force-fed a check can be made by gently feeling the bulge of its crop; this is the swelling at the base of the throat.

Obviously, if the chick needs an insect diet (this type of juvenile is far the most common among garden birds) you will need to find an abundance of houseflies, moths, caterpillars and other soft-bodied larvae. The insects must be killed first and, with a pair of tweezers, pushed well down the chick's throat. If this is not done it will probably not swallow the food. Small pieces of raw minced meat may be used to supplement the insect diet, but too much of this will deprive the bird of the natural vitamins it needs. Normally young insect- and fruit-eating birds do not need water since they obtain the necessary moisture from their food. Should you have an irresistible urge to give it water simply administer a single drop into the open beak. Containers with water merely get trodden in and the chick's plumage becomes messy.

With young doves or pigeons the task of feeding them is even more difficult and less appetising. Initially, in their natural state, young birds of this family are fed on 'pigeon's milk' which is produced internally by the parent. Later they are given regurgitated semi-digested seeds. This must be substituted with a mixture of seeds, mealie pap, millet and whole-wheat bread all crushed to a fine consistency and well soaked in water. To this add the smallest amount of bone-meal. The whole-wheat bread should, ideally, be well chewed and mixed with human saliva before it is added to the mash. This mixture should be given to the bird in a small spoon with the fist closed over it so that the young bird can push its bill between spoon and fingers to get at the meal. This simulates the action of putting its bill into that of its mother. The mixture should be fairly wet because, unlike other birds, doves and pigeons need plenty of water.

Should you find yourself in charge of a young heron, bird of prey or any large bird you may only need to feed it twice a day, but here again its normal diet must be carefully checked. Many of these young larger birds will need a certain amount of roughage with their meat in the form of fur and hair, such as they would get under natural conditions. A good substitute is the combings of a dog's coat wrapped around the food before it is offered. It is also advisable to give them a small amount of vitamins A and D daily with their food to prevent rickets, but consult your veterinary surgeon about the correct dosages.

Young birds should be encouraged to pick up food for themselves the moment they are able to do so, and the sooner this is learned, the sooner one can dispense with the tedium of hand-feeding. Likewise it is important to encourage them to fly at the earliest opportunity. If a small bird has made proper progress it should be independent within a month.

Careful attention should be given to a young bird's living quarters. A box well lined with newspapers is best, and this should be kept in a draught-free place out of the sun. Daylight is necessary to make it feed. Darkness will make it sleep. One of the more important points is the maintenance of cleanliness in the box to prevent the young bird from soiling its plumage with droppings. In natural circumstances the young bird, after being fed, raises its posterior and expels its excreta within a thin membranous capsule called the faecal sac. This sac is seized by the parent and discarded well away from the nest. The duty of the foster-parent is to remove these faecal sacs as soon as they come, to keep the box clean.

When the bird is old enough to stand it should be given a perch. At this stage its droppings are of a different consistency and are no longer encased in a faecal sac. The newspapers should then be changed the moment they are soiled. A good alternative is to make a false floor to the box with a layer of chicken wire. The droppings will then fall through onto the paper beneath, leaving the box clean.

Young birds of prey maintain nest cleanliness by lifting their behinds and ejecting their excreta through the air with considerable force. These birds should be given a low-sided box encircled by a carpet of newspapers to a distance of about two metres.

Casualties among adult birds

If you are able to pick up a wild bird it is clearly in need of help. On no account chase the bird in order to 'rescue' it. When handling a bird allow it to rest or perch on your hand and merely place a restraining hand lightly over its back. If the bird is injured take it to a veterinary surgeon for proper treatment. Do not attempt this yourself.

Frequently casualties are suffering from slight concussion through colliding with something. Put the bird in a large, draught-free box, with papers at the bottom and something steady for it to perch on. Place the appropriate food near to it (although it will probably not eat) plus a little water in a receptacle, then leave it in a quiet place to rest, preferably with dim light. Do not force it to eat and do not give it brandy. More than likely it will be able to fly away the next day.

When you see a cat or dog with a bird in its mouth it is often possible to rescue the victim by firmly pressing the animal's jaws at the side of its face, at the point where they hinge. This will cause its mouth to open and the bird can be retrieved. It is important that the assailant be handled calmly and quickly; any grabbing or chasing may cause it to bite its victim harder. Many birds seem to be undamaged by the experience and are able to fly almost immediately. Others may be only slightly hurt or suffering from shock, and these should be treated in the manner already described.

It must be pointed out that the keeping of most wild birds is illegal without a permit from the local nature conservancy. Should you need to care for a young or injured bird for a prolonged period (say in excess of four weeks) be sure to telephone your nearest Department of Nature Conservation and explain the position. You will find them very understanding and co-operative.

How to use this book

The birds described on the following pages may be expected to occur commonly at some time of the year in the average suburban garden of at least one of the cities or towns shown on the map opposite. Only birds that habitually enter gardens are included.

The term 'average suburban garden' refers to one comprising a half hectare or less, surrounded by properties of similar size. Gardens that border on rivers, forests, indigenous bush or open veld will probably be visited by the birds unique to those habitats and cannot, therefore, be treated as average suburban gardens.

The illustrations have been painted to indicate as clearly as possible the most important visual characteristics of each species: colour, markings, shape and stance. In this new edition photographs have been included to further help with identification and to emphasise certain behaviours of the birds concerned. Many of the birds described are very small, some smaller than a sparrow; it is therefore important to realise that some form of visual aid is necessary when looking at them at any distance. A yellow bird may appear grey or brown beyond 10 metres, or in poor light, while eye-stripes and breast colouring may not be seen at all at such distances. The reader is therefore advised to acquire a pair of binoculars.

A wide range of binoculars is available these days, at varying prices. Resist the temptation to buy a very cheap pair or one with a very powerful magnification. The first may harm your eyes, while the second will probably be too heavy to hold steady. Look for something marked in the region of 7×30, 8×35, 9×40 or 10×40. The first figure indicates the magnification, while the second is the diameter of the front lens expressed in millimetres, and is therefore an indication of the amount of light admitted by the front or objective lens. The larger the front lens the brighter the image seen.

When scrutinising a bird first look at it without binoculars. Then, without taking your gaze from it, place the binoculars to the eyes and focus. This will be found much easier than searching a wide area with the binoculars. With a little practice on inanimate objects the technique will soon be mastered.

On seeing an unfamiliar bird in your garden exercise the habit of checking it in a systematic manner. The following example may be found useful:
1. Estimate the size in comparison to a sparrow. If it seems larger than a sparrow (a sparrow measures about 150 mm beak to tail), then check it against a pigeon.
2. Note the shape and colour of its beak. (This is a good clue to the sort of bird it is.)
3. Note the length and colour of its legs; is there anything unusual about them?
4. Note its general colouring and special features: long tail, crested head, prominent colours or markings.

5. Note the bird's behaviour: pecking on the lawn, eating fruit, running up the trunk of a tree, scrambling about in foliage, etc.
6. Should the bird be calling try to make a mental note of the sound, or write it down. Having done these things turn the colour pages until you see an illustration that compares with what you have seen. Next, check the distribution map on that page to see if the bird occurs in your area. If so, then check the silhouette on that page to see how the illustrated bird compares to the size of a sparrow. Finally, assuming that its size, appearance and distribution accord with the book, check the text for further helpful details, including its call if that was heard.

For each species described, following its name in large type, its national number appears in small type. This is intended as an aid when checking the bird in other books. Likewise any other names by which it may be known, including its Afrikaans and scientific names, are given.

Basic key-map

The cities and towns on this map are those with a population of 20 000 or more. For purposes of simplification the Johannesburg mark should be regarded as including the entire Reef from Springs to Krugersdorp. Likewise the mark for Cape Town covers Bellville.

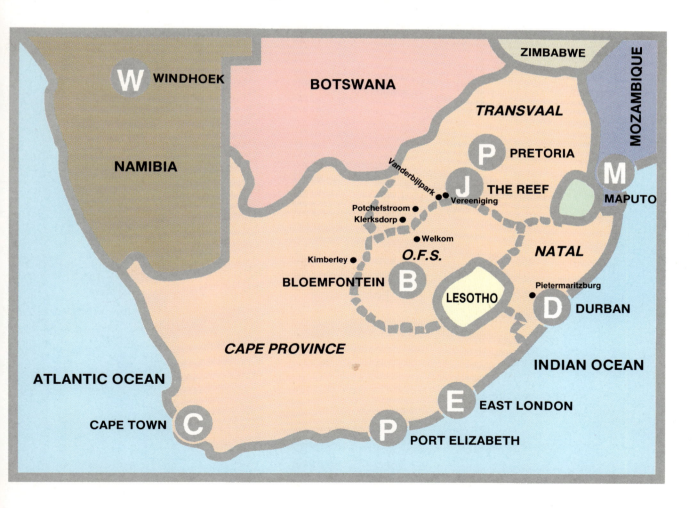

The small reproductions of this map which appear on the following pages have been simplified by the omission of certain town names, while those that do appear on them are keyed by the initial letter of the town; thus 'B' signifies Bloemfontein. The bird distributions shown in colour on the page maps are approximate, and are intended as a guide only. Obviously any bird is likely to be seen in any part of its distribution area outside of the towns marked.

Birds' eggs

Photographs of the eggs of the various garden species have been included for the first time in this edition. They serve as an additional feature of interest and as a guide to the identity of the owners of nests, and of egg shells found. Following egg-hatching the shells are normally discarded by the parent birds, and may be found lying in the garden.

A warning

It must be stressed that the collecting or possession of wild bird's eggs is illegal, and can carry heavy penalties. The eggs photographed for this book are from the collection of the Bird Department, Transvaal Museum, Pretoria, and my thanks are due to the Director and staff for their valuable assistance.

Descriptions of Birds

Hamerkop

NATIONAL NUMBER 81

VOICE
The Hamerkop makes a strange nasal 'wek . . . wek . . . wek . . . wek . . .' in flight. It may also make a high-pitched, wavering 'wek-wek-warrrrrk' repeatedly while at rest.

OTHER NAMES
LIGHTNING BIRD
Scopus umbretta

The Hamerkop is found on rivers and dams throughout South Africa.

This largish, all-brown bird with its strange, backwards-projecting crest and long black legs is unmistakable and well known as a bird of inland waterways. Yet, in many urban areas close to rivers the Hamerkop becomes a regular fish pond visitor, especially in the cooler months. At the fish pond it is mainly interested in frogs, but will certainly seize a fish if it can. Often, in order to flush out its prey, it will walk quickly across floating lily leaves, then suddenly turn around to see if anything has been disturbed. The sexes are alike.

The Hamerkop normally feeds in shallow rivers, dams and rain puddles where it catches small fish, frogs and tadpoles.

NESTING

The Hamerkop's nest must be the largest of any bird in Africa. A massive dome of sticks, reeds and assorted debris measuring some one and a half metres across and placed in the fork of a large tree or on a rock near water. The nest has a mud-plastered side entrance facing outwards and downwards, and leading to an inner mud-plastered chamber where up to five eggs are laid. Breeding may occur at any time of the year but the warmer months tend to be favoured. Both sexes share in the 28–32 day incubation period and in the care of the nestlings, which leave the nest about 45 days after hatching.

The Hamerkop usually chooses a tree for its nest.

A bird's-eye view of a Hamerkop's nest situated on a rock. In addition to the usual materials, paper and plastic bags have been used.

The smooth white eggs of the Hamerkop sometimes become stained brown. They average 46 mm in length.

IN THE GARDEN

Any garden pond is likely to attract the Hamerkop provided that it contains frogs or fish; it will not eat other food. Favoured visiting times are the early hours of the morning, and it will often herald its approach by calling in flight. At other times it will arrive silently and may spend much time in the pond without being detected.

Hadeda Ibis

NATIONAL NUMBER 94

OTHER NAMES
HADEDA
Bostrychia hagedash

This large bird has entered urban areas in many parts of the country and has become a frequent garden visitor in some regions. It forages about in flower beds, on lawns and in compost heaps, probing the ground with its long curved bill in search of subterranean insects and their larvae. It does not eat seeds or plants and so is a useful ally to the gardener and soon becomes remarkably tolerant of human presence. An unmistakable bird, its size and bill shape plus, in good light, a bright, coppery-pink sheen on the folded wing revealing its identity. The sexes are alike. Usually occurs in small flocks.

VOICE
If the Hadeda cannot be identified by size, bill shape and colouring then its voice, once heard, will leave nothing to doubt. Its name is a rough onomatopoeic rendering of its raucous call 'haaa, haa-de-daa' or simply 'haaaa' given at take-off or in flight. When the call is heard at daybreak (as it often is) and uttered by a passing flock there is little hope of continued sleep! The Hadeda Ibis must be the noisiest bird in Africa.

LEFT *The Hadeda at its nest, which is typically placed in a tree over water.*

BELOW *The chicks are fed by regurgitation, the young bird inserting its bill inside that of its parent.*

NESTING

The Hadeda breeds July–January, building a flimsy stick platform on a horizontal branch of a tree, often over water. Two to four eggs are laid and incubated by both sexes for up to 28 days. The chicks are nest-bound for about 36 days although they usually wander about the branches of the tree during the latter stages. They finally become fully independent of their parents at about 50 days. At this stage they have a straight, not curved, bill.

The Hadeda's eggs vary between whitish or yellowish, well marked with brown smudges. The average egg length is 61 mm.

IN THE GARDEN

It is unlikely that Hadedas will visit garden bird tables but, provided they are resident in an urban district, will visit the average large garden to forage, and may perch on trees, walls and rooftops. They have little to fear from cats but are frequently chased by dogs.

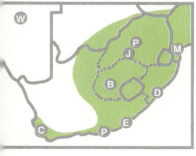

The Hadeda Ibis has a mainly easterly and southerly distribution, being absent from the dry west. However, within its known range it may be patchily distributed, preferring the moister regions, especially well-watered farmlands and river banks.

Rock Pigeon

NATIONAL NUMBER 349

OTHER NAMES
SPECKLED PIGEON
Kransduif; Bosduif
Columba guinea

This large bird, roughly the size of the common town pigeon or racing pigeon, is by far the largest pigeon likely to be seen in most gardens. The dull reddish plumage with prominent white spots plus the grey head and patch of red skin surrounding the yellow eye are distinctive. The sexes are alike.

Away from towns the Rock Pigeon roosts and breeds on rocky cliffs. However, it enters towns readily where houses and other man-made structures are accepted as substitute cliffs. It will take up residence on any convenient ledge, gutter or rooftop and raise its young there.

VOICE
The call of the Rock Pigeon is a resonant, mellow cooing 'doo, doo, doo'.

NESTING

In common with that of most pigeons the nest is a simple platform of twigs placed on a rock ledge, rooftop, roof gutter or wooden beam. (Nests built entirely of wire have been found in industrial regions.) Two eggs are laid. Incubation is by both parents and lasts about 14 days; thereafter the chick remains in the nest for another 26 days while both parents continue to feed and care for it.

A Rock Pigeon on its nest in the gutter of a house.

This Rock Pigeon has squeezed its nest between the roof and a beam of a stable.

The pure white eggs of the Rock Pigeon are on average 36,5 mm in length.

IN THE GARDEN

Rock Pigeons do not usually feed in gardens although they can be enticed with a plentiful daily supply of grain; like others of their family, they will drink at permanent water. Normally they prefer to fly daily to agricultural lands, often covering considerable distances to get there. They fly high and directly in flocks of up to 30 birds. On arrival at their feeding grounds, the converging flocks may number many hundreds of birds which can do great damage to grain crops.

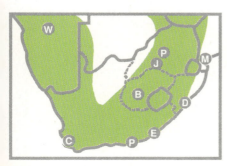

The Rock Pigeon is found throughout South Africa with the exception of the northern Cape, being most plentiful in mountainous regions.

Cape Turtle Dove and Redeyed Dove

NATIONAL NUMBERS RESPECTIVELY 354 AND 352

OTHER NAMES: CAPE TURTLE DOVE
RINGNECKED DOVE
Gewone Tortelduif
Streptopelia capicola

OTHER NAMES: REDEYED DOVE
RINGNECKED DOVE
Grootringduif
Streptopelia semitorquata

VOICE OF CAPE TURTLE DOVE
The characteristic call resembles the words 'work HARDER, work HARDER' or 'tell FATHER, tell FATHER', much repeated. On settling in a tree it makes a harsh, high-pitched 'kerrr' several times.

Superficially these two doves are very similar, with black collar-bands, black bills and red legs, their specific differences becoming apparent only on closer study.

The Cape Turtle Dove is the smaller of the two and is greyer although the depth of colour is variable, ranging from pale grey to sooty on the wings. In flight, especially on take-off, the tail can be seen to be white-tipped.

In urban gardens we normally see the Cape Turtle Dove foraging for food singly, but in country districts they often form large flocks.

The Cape Turtle Dove is widespread throughout the country, occurring in even the driest regions. It is common in most urban areas except East London.

The Redeyed Dove is 25% larger than the Cape Turtle Dove, the black collar is wider, the eye is red with a variable surround of bare red flesh while the body plumage is a dark purplish grey becoming noticeably pink about the face and breast, this contrasting with the grey cap. In flight the tail shows no white. The general habits and food requirements of the Redeyed Dove are essentially the same as those of the Cape Turtle Dove, although the former tends to perch in taller trees.

VOICE OF REDEYED DOVE
The call is a much repeated 'coo-coo, coo-CUK-coo-coo', the accent being on the fourth syllable. It can be likened to the words 'Father, why DON'T you work' or 'I am, a RED-eyed dove'.

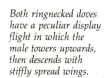

Both ringnecked doves have a peculiar display flight in which the male towers upwards, then descends with stiffly spread wings.

Here the red eye, red eye-ring and pinkish tinge to the breast plumage are evident. Photo: Peter Steyn.

NESTING
The nests of both Cape Turtle and Redeyed Doves are simple platforms of sticks built at almost any time of the year and placed in a bush or tree. Two eggs are laid and are incubated by both sexes for up to 17 days. The nestlings are fed by regurgitation and will fledge at 16–20 days, being dependent on the parents for another two weeks.

RINGNECKED DOVES IN THE GARDEN
While the Redeyed Dove is the shyer of the two, both doves will frequent bird tables but prefer to take their food from the ground. Their normal diet consists of grain, seeds and insects and they will respond readily to offerings of the first two items plus bread, mealie pap and dog food. They need water daily.

Both doves lay pure white eggs. Those of the Cape Turtle Dove (left) average 28 mm in length, while those of the Redeyed Dove (right) average 31 mm.

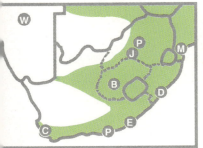

The distribution of the Redeyed Dove extends from the western Cape eastwards and northwards to the Limpopo River, being absent only from the northern Cape and west-central regions.

Laughing Dove

NATIONAL NUMBER 355

OTHER NAMES
SENEGAL DOVE
Rooiborsduifie; Lemoenduifie
Streptopelia senegalensis

VOICE
The soft call of the Laughing Dove is one of the characteristic sounds of our countryside, and is heard almost continually on warm days. A gently bubbling 'cooroocoo-kuk-coo'.

This attractive little dove with its dappled lilac-grey and cinnamon-brown plumage can be told immediately from other common garden doves (see previous pages) by the *lack* of a black collar. The plumage is soft and the body contour feathers fall out easily. The sexes are identical.

The Laughing Dove feeds on the ground in a hunched posture, moving about with slow, shuffling steps in search of seeds and insects. The take-off is characterised by a squeaking sound made by the wings. In courtship the male approaches the female with hunched back and raised feathers while making exaggerated bows; whereupon she normally flies away!

The Laughing Dove is very common and widespread throughout the country, although its distribution is patchy in some regions. It also occurs over much of Africa north of the Limpopo River.

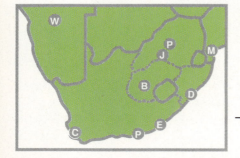

ABOVE *A Laughing Dove incubating its eggs on a typically flimsy nest.*
BELOW *A newly hatched chick with one unhatched egg.*

NESTING
The Laughing Dove breeds at any time of the year, the nest being a simple platform of sticks placed in a bush or tree. Two eggs are laid and incubated by both sexes for up to 16 days. The nestlings, initially naked and blind, are fed by regurgitation and usually leave the nest at about 12 days, but will sometimes do so prematurely.

In common with most members of its family the Laughing Dove lays pure white eggs. They are on average 26 mm in length.

IN THE GARDEN
Laughing Doves can become very numerous in gardens where a regular food supply is available. They come readily to bird tables, often being the first to arrive and the last to leave. Although basically granivorous they may be attracted also by bread, mealie pap, dog food, bone-meal, cheese and a variety of other kitchen scraps but will seldom eat fruit. They prefer a stable feeding table but will usually glean the fallen scraps below it. They need water daily.

Grey Lourie

NATIONAL NUMBER 373

OTHER NAMES
GO-AWAY BIRD
Kwêvoël
Corythaixoides concolor

VOICE
The call of the Grey Lourie is 'kweh-h-h-h' or 'go-way-y-y-y', hence its popular name. Young birds call 'how, how . . .'.

Well known as the Go-away Bird this all-grey lourie, with its crested head and familiar call, is unmistakable, and the sexes are alike. It has long been a regular garden visitor in country towns of the northern Transvaal, also living in many of Pretoria's wooded suburbs. However, since about the mid-1970s the Grey Lourie has increased its range southwards into the Highveld proper, and is now a common breeding resident in Sandton and the northern suburbs of Johannesburg. What was once treeless grassveld is today well-wooded suburbia; a good example of the benefit to some birds of man-made environmental changes.

The Grey Lourie is usually seen in pairs or small family groups in gardens with large trees, in which they move with a springy, bouncing action. They fly with laboured wing-beats alternating with glides.

NESTING
A simple platform nest of sticks is built within a dense tree canopy or matted creeper well above ground. Two or three eggs are laid and are incubated by both sexes for up to 28 days. The young are fed by both parents and leave the nest after about 20 days but do not fly at least until their 40th day, being fed the while by both parents and the grown young of a previous brood.

Grey Louries feeding on pawpaw skins at a bird table.

The eggs of the Grey Lourie are usually white, occasionally tinted yellow or bluish, and on average 41,5 mm in length.

IN THE GARDEN
Its liking for soft fruits makes the Grey Lourie a ready visitor to bird tables; its preference being for pawpaws, apples, pears and grapes. Because of its large size and the real likelihood of several louries coming to feed at once, a stable platform should be provided, preferably with a raised edge since the food tends to get knocked to the ground. For the same reason it is wise to impale apples, pears, etc. on a large nail protruding from the base of the table.

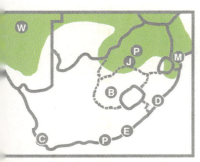

The Grey Lourie is found throughout the Transvaal except for the south-eastern and south-western regions; it is also found in northern Zululand.

Redchested Cuckoo

NATIONAL NUMBER 377

OTHER NAMES
Piet-my-vrou
Cuculus solitarius

VOICE
The Afrikaans name Piet-my-vrou is an onomatopoeic rendering of the call of the Redchested Cuckoo, which can otherwise be described as 'whip-whip-whoo' repeated loudly and frequently. The newly fledged young calls 'seep, seep, seep . . .'.

This dove-sized cuckoo with its russet breast and banded underparts is best identified by its well-known call, which gives rise to its alternative name; much used in both English and Afrikaans. The Redchested Cuckoo arrives in the country during October, and the male is highly vocal for the next few months. It calls from a high tree for protracted periods, often at night, but is difficult to locate. It also calls in flight, at which time it resembles a small bird of prey. When not calling it is easily overlooked.

The distribution of the Redchested Cuckoo, dependent as it is on the presence of suitable host species, ranges along a broad coastal belt from the western to the eastern Cape, also spreading westerly and northerly.

NESTING

In common with all true cuckoos the Redchested is a brood parasite, laying its eggs in the nests of robins, chats, wagtails and others. The female cuckoo deposits its egg very soon after the first egg of its host has been laid. The cuckoo egg, which has an incubation time as short as 12 days, invariably hatches before the others, whereupon the young cuckoo, blind and featherless, evicts the eggs or young of the host. The young cuckoo develops rapidly and leaves the nest at between 18 and 22 days at which time it usually dwarfs its foster parents.

The chocolate brown egg of the Redchested Cuckoo often does not match that of its host. Here it is seen with the eggs of the Cape Robin. The cuckoo egg averages 24,6 mm in length.

IN THE GARDEN

The Redchested Cuckoo cannot be attracted to the garden with food since it eats mostly hairy caterpillars, but it can be attracted by the mid-summer infestations of caterpillars that invariably attack the indigenous tree *Kiggelaria africana*: see under this heading for the Diederik Cuckoo (following pages).

On leaving the nest the fledgeling cuckoo is dark grey overall except for white underparts finely barred.

The nest of a Cape Robin containing two speckled robin eggs and one plain brown egg of the Redchested Cuckoo. Hatching before the young robins, the blind cuckoo chick's first impulse is to evict other objects from the nest.

With flattened back the young cuckoo manoeuvres the host's egg between its wing-stubs and slowly pushes itself up the side of the nest.

The young cuckoo, ever ready to accept more food, grows quickly with the undivided attention of its foster parents.

At about 18 days the cuckoo is ready to fledge.

Diederik Cuckoo

NATIONAL NUMBER 386

OTHER NAMES
Diederikkie
Chrysococcyx caprius

VOICE
The plaintive call of the male Diederik is one of the common sounds of a summer's day, a high-pitched, far-carrying 'dee, dee, deederik' rising then falling in pitch and much repeated. The female calls less often 'deea-deea-deea'. Both sexes call in flight and at rest. The young utter a continuous 'peep-peep-peep-peep . . .'.

The young, recently fledged Diederik Cuckoo has a pink bill and blue eyes.

The Diederik Cuckoo may be found throughout the country, its occurrence everywhere dictated by the presence of its host species.

This emerald-green and white, bulbul-sized cuckoo, a common summer visitor, is best identified by its call. The reason is that despite its bright iridescent colouring the Diederik Cuckoo is not easily located unless in flight, when it often draws attention to itself by calling. The female is similar to the male but is usually more coppery on the back.

The Diederik Cukoo arrives about late September and is with us until March. During this time the male is very noisy, calling for much of the day and chasing other males. It may also be seen feeding caterpillars in courtship to the female.

The juvenile Diederik Cuckoo is coppery in colour.

NESTING
The Diederik Cuckoo is a brood parasite, laying its eggs in the nest of another bird. Favourite hosts are weavers, bishop birds and Cape Sparrows, all of which build enclosed nests, but other species have also been recorded. The female Diederik lays a single egg in the chosen nest, removing and eating one egg of the host. Frequently the female is vigorously attacked by the host species while attempting to enter the nest and may be driven to the ground, even killed.

The young Diederik Cuckoo hatches after 10–12 days, usually in advance of its foster siblings, ejecting all other eggs and young from the nest. It is fed and reared by its hosts within the nest for about 20 days and for as much as 32 days after fledging.

EGG-MATCHING
An intriguing sidelight on the parasitism of the Diederik Cuckoo is its apparent ability to closely match its eggs to the colour of the eggs of its host. Studies carried out both in southern Africa and overseas suggest that each female specialises on one host species, or perhaps a few closely related species with similar breeding habits, probably the same species by which she herself was reared.

In the above photograph the three spotted eggs on the left are those of a Masked Weaver, that of the cuckoo being on the right. Below are three blue eggs of a Spottedbacked Weaver with (lower right) the closely matching egg of the Diederik Cuckoo parasite. Diederik Cuckoo eggs average 18,6 mm in length.

A cutaway nest of a Masked Weaver into which the parasitised contents of another Masked Weaver's nest have been placed to show the Diederik Cuckoo chick in the act of evicting the smaller chick of its host. Photo: Peter Steyn.

IN THE GARDEN
Most cuckoos, including the Diederik, feed mainly on caterpillars. It is therefore not possible to attract them to a bird table. On the other hand they may be temporarily attracted to the garden during December–January by the presence of the tree *Kiggelaria africana* which becomes heavily infested with a blackish, hairy caterpillar at this time.

Burchell's Coucal

NATIONAL NUMBER 391

OTHER NAMES
RAIN BIRD
Gewone Vleiloerie
Centropus superciliosus

This crow-sized, chestnut, black and white bird is secretive, skulking in dense vegetation. It favours reedbeds in vleis, dams and rivers but enters gardens where adequate cover is present. It will venture onto lawns in the early hours of the morning and in the late evening or may sun itself on an exposed branch after rain, but is more often heard than seen despite its large size. Burchell's Coucal normally occurs in pairs which keep in touch with frequent calling.

Burchell's Coucal occurs throughout most of the Transvaal and in the coastal belt from Zululand to the western Cape.

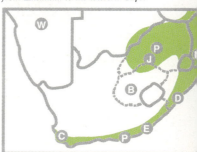

VOICE
The distinctive call of Burchell's Coucal is a series of liquid hooting notes first descending the scale then rising 'doo, doo, doo-doo-doo-doodoodoodoodoodoodoo', like the sound of liquid pouring from a bottle, often given by a pair in duet. It also makes a harsh, grating alarm call.

A Burchell's Coucal at its bulky grass nest.

The eggs of Burchell's Coucal are white, with a coarse texture, each averaging 33,6 mm in length.

NESTING
Burchell's Coucal builds a large, loosely constructed ball-shaped nest of grasses and reeds with an entrance at one end. This is placed fairly low in matted vegetation. Four eggs are usually laid and incubation lasts about 16 days. The nestlings, which are initially all-black, fledge at 18–20 days — before they are able to fly properly — and are fed by the parents for some days afterwards.

NOTE: If a newly fledged young coucal is found it should be placed carefully in some dense bush nearby, away from domestic animals. Its parents will then respond to its calls and continue to feed it. It should on no account be moved far from where it was first found.

IN THE GARDEN
Burchell's Coucal is an ally of the gardener since it eats snails. It will occasionally visit bird tables, especially when regular offerings of bone-meal are available. The natural diet of this species is insects, snails, small frogs and other reptiles, nestling birds and small rodents.

Three newly fledged Burchell's Coucals await the arrival of the next meal.

Barn Owl
NATIONAL NUMBER 392

OTHER NAMES
Nonnetjie-uil
Tyto alba

This is a medium-sized owl, about 32 cm in length. Very pale in colour, it lacks the 'ear-tufts' of many owls, the distinctive heart-shaped face and whitish underparts being diagnostic. The sexes are alike.

By day the Barn Owl roosts in some darkened out-building, attic, hole in a tree or the base of a palm frond. By night it quarters the ground in low, silent flight, searching for small rodents, small roosting birds, frogs and insects. Though common in many towns it is seldom seen, but its eerie call can often be heard in the hours of darkness.

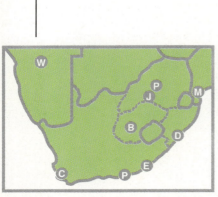

The Barn Owl is found throughout the country in a wide variety of habitats, including very dry regions, provided suitable roosts and nest sites are available. It avoids evergreen forests.

VOICE
The call of the Barn Owl, frequently made while it is flying as well as at rest, is a prolonged, wheezy screech 'schreeeeee'. In defence of its nest it will hiss at the intruder.

Away from urban areas the Barn Owl frequently roosts and nests inside a Hamerkop's nest. In this picture the Barn Owl is approaching the entrance hole.

NESTING
The Barn Owl constructs no nest but lays its eggs on whatever level surface is available within its choosen roost, the same site being used repeatedly if undisturbed. The number of eggs in the clutch varies according to food availability; normally it is 3–9 but this number may rise when rodents are plentiful. Each egg requires 32 days of incubation but, since the female commences incubation with the first egg, the chicks hatch at intervals. The nestlings fledge after 45–55 days.

Barn Owl chicks in their nest. The Barn Owl starts incubation when the first egg is laid, hence the disparity in the sizes of the chicks. Photo: Peter Steyn.

The somewhat rounded, chalky-white eggs of the Barn Owl have an average length of 40,7 mm.

IN THE GARDEN
The Barn Owl cannot be attracted by food but will sometimes accept a specially made roosting and nesting box. This should be a wooden box with inside dimensions of approximately 50 × 30 cm and a depth of about 20 cm, preferably with a sloping roof. In one end of the box a central hole of 10 cm diameter should be made. The outside of the finished product should be treated against the weather, and the box nailed securely, with supporting planks if necessary, on a high branch of a tree next to the trunk.

The Barn Owl's plumage is a subtle mixture of pale fawn and purple-grey, but when seen at night it appears white.

Spotted Eagle Owl

NATIONAL NUMBER 401

OTHER NAMES
Gevlekte Ooruil
Bubo africanus

When it knows that it is being watched a roosting Spotted Eagle Owl will sleek its plumage, raise its 'ear-tufts' and half close its eyes, taking on a thin look to resemble the branch of a tree.

The Spotted Eagle Owl is the largest owl to regularly frequent urban areas, measuring as it does 58–65 cm in length. A greyish owl with finely barred and blotched underparts, prominent 'ear-tufts' and pale yellow eyes.

In spite of its formidable appearance the Spotted Eagle Owl feeds mostly on beetles, mice and small birds, becoming active at dusk. During the day it roosts in a leafy tree or among rocks. On clear nights it may be seen perched on rooftops, gate posts or in roads, where it is often run down by cars.

With its eyes wide open the Spotted Eagle Owl has a fierce expression.

These Spotted Eagle Owls have nested in a window box, a favourite site. Photo: Peter Steyn.

VOICE
These owls often call in duet, a low 'hooooo, hu', the second note much softer. Single birds call 'hooo-hoo' or 'hoo-hoohoo'.

NESTING
In an urban situation the eggs of the Spotted Eagle Owl may be placed on the ground among rocks, on the ledge of a building or at the base of a large branch in a tree, bluegum trees being favoured. The breeding season is May–January and normally two eggs are laid. These are incubated by the female for 30–32 days; a nestling period of about 40 days follows. Once fledged the chicks are fed by their parents for another five weeks.

The Spotted Eagle Owl lays smooth white eggs with an average length of 49,5 mm.

IN THE GARDEN
It is not normally possible to attract owls to the garden with food but a pair of Spotted Eagle Owls may take up residence if large trees are present, especially bluegums. However, because of their nocturnal way of life their presence in a district may often go undetected. When they are known to be around it is possible to provide a nest site by placing an open wooden box securely on a branch of a tree. The box should measure about 60 × 45 cm and be about 23 cm in depth.

The Spotted Eagle Owl is widespread throughout the country and is present in most towns with tall trees.

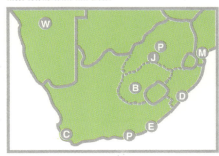

Greater and Lesser Striped Swallows

NATIONAL NUMBERS RESPECTIVELY 526 AND 527

OTHER NAMES: GREATER STRIPED SWALLOW
Grootstreepswael
Hirundo cucullata

OTHER NAMES: LESSER STRIPED SWALLOW
Kleinstreepswael
Hirundo abyssinica

VOICES OF STRIPED SWALLOWS
The characteristic in-flight calls of both species serve as a good guide to their identification. In the case of the Greater this is a soft 'chissik' while that of the Lesser is a four-syllabled, descending 'eh-eh-eh-eh'.

Both striped swallows are present in and around our gardens for much of the year, migrating to central Africa for two to three months during winter. Their similarity is a cause of much confusion. The simplest rule to remember is that the Greater Striped Swallow, which is the larger (about 20 cm in length), has the sides of the head, including the ear coverts, *white*, only the crown and nape being chestnut in colour. In the Lesser Striped Swallow (about 16 cm in length) the chestnut of the crown *extends over the ear coverts*. Other points are that the Greater has only very narrow black streaks on its underparts while the rump is *pale* chestnut in colour; the Lesser has its underparts densely marked in heavy black streaks and its rump is a rich chestnut.

A Greater Striped Swallow leaving its nest. Photo: Peter Steyn.

NESTING

In both species the nest is plastered under the roof or eaves and consists of a mud chamber resembling an inverted bowl with a fairly long tubular entrance on one side. Three eggs are usually laid within the chamber and incubated for about 16 days in the Greater and 14 days in the Lesser Striped Swallow. The Greater Striped Swallow chicks remain in the nest for 23–30 days and thereafter return to it to roost for another ten days. Chicks of the Lesser Striped Swallow spend about 18 days in the nest and also return at night initially after fledging. Both species may have two or three broods in a season and will use the same site year after year.

Lesser Striped Swallows repairing their nest. Photo: Peter Steyn.

The nest of a Lesser Striped Swallow with a particularly long entrance spout.

Both striped swallows lay pure white eggs. Those of the Lesser Striped Swallow (left) measure about 20 mm in length and those of the Greater (right) 22,5 mm.

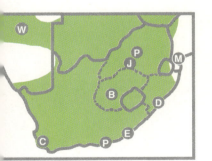

Greater Striped Swallows (above) occur throughout the country, being most common at higher altitudes, while Lesser Striped Swallows (below) occur in the east, mostly at lower altitudes.

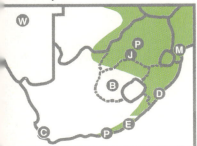

IN THE GARDEN

Since swallows eat flying insects caught on the wing it is not possible to attract them to a bird table. On the other hand striped swallows can be encouraged to build nests by supplying mud. A well-watered mud-patch under a garden tap will provide them with the necessary building material and will prove especially welcome during dry weather.

Should young swallows leave their nest prematurely the cause may be an infestation of ants or bird lice, or they may have been evicted by another bird. Provided they are feathered the chicks should be placed on a safe, protected perch and left alone, after which the parents will probably continue to feed them.

Whiterumped Swift and Little Swift

NATIONAL NUMBER 415

NATIONAL NUMBER 417

OTHER NAMES: WHITERUMPED SWIFT
Witkruiswindswael
Apus caffer

VOICE
Swifts are normally silent except when feeding or near their roosts at which time they make shrill screams.

OTHER NAMES: LITTLE SWIFT
INDIAN SWIFT
Kleinwindswael
Apus affinis

Both Whiterumped and Little Swifts occur throughout South Africa, being present from about August to April, sometimes later in the Little Swift, both migrating northwards for the winter months.

Although both swifts occur throughout the country they generally go unnoticed because of their aerial way of life. Both species, however, commonly breed in towns. Both are basically blackish-brown birds, the Whiterumped being slightly the larger with a length of 15 cm against the Little Swift's 14 cm. Both have whitish throat patches but, while the Whiterumped is told by a forked tail and crescent-shaped white patch on its rump, the Little Swift has a square tail and a large, rectangular white rump-patch that wraps around its flanks.

Swifts are in no way related to swallows. They cannot perch and, should they accidentally become grounded, their long wings and short legs make it very difficult for them to get airborne again. When swifts wish to rest they cling to a rock face or wall or enter some rock fissure or similar ledge in a man-made structure. They spend most of the daylight hours in high-speed flight, feeding on airborne insects, often at great height.

Swifts cannot perch but cling to a vertical surface to rest, their claws being particularly long and sharp for this purpose.

A Little Swift building a nest. A bowl of feathers and grass fragments is cemented with saliva to an overhang with many nests close together. All material for nest construction is gathered in flight.

NESTING

The Whiterumped Swift in an urban environment will either nest in the eaves or use the mud nest of a striped swallow, evicting the owners. The swallow's nest is then lined with feathers. Two eggs are usually laid and are incubated by both parents for up to 26 days. The chicks will remain in the nest 53 days or more.

The Little Swift breeds colonially, each pair constructing a bowl-shaped nest of feathers and grass with a small side entrance. It is attached to a rock overhang or, in an urban situation, under a window recess or similar ledge, with many nests in close proximity. Two to three eggs are laid and hatch at about 22 days, the chicks fledging at 36–40 days. Both swifts may have two or three broods in a season.

Because of the extremely aerial way of life of the swift a young bird will not normally fledge until it is fully developed and able to fly well since, once on the wing, it must be able to keep up with the flock and feed itself.

For this reason a swift's nestling period is unusually long, and may be further prolonged by poor weather.

IN THE GARDEN

There is no way in which swifts can be attracted to the garden. Their presence as breeding species also cannot be influenced in any way, but the existence of striped swallows' nests is often an attraction for the Whiterumped Swift.

The eggs of both swifts are white and elongated. The Whiterumped Swift's eggs (right) vary in length between 16,2 mm and 26,1 mm. Those of the Little Swift vary between 15,3 mm and 25,4 mm.

Whitebacked and Speckled Mousebirds

NATIONAL NUMBERS RESPECTIVELY 425 AND 424

OTHER NAMES: WHITEBACKED MOUSEBIRD
WHITEBACKED COLY
Witkruismuisvoël
Colius colius

Although the Whitebacked Mousebird has a white back this is seldom seen unless the bird is flying. This mousebird is best told by its bluish-white bill with black tip and grey upperparts, only the lower breast and belly being buffy. Its feet are bright red; the sexes alike.

The Speckled Mousebird is entirely rusty brown except for a slight darkening of the throat and breast. Its name is derived from the fine barring on its breast. Again the bill colour is diagnostic, being black above and bluish-white below; the region surrounding the eyes is blackish while the feet are dull red. The sexes are alike.

The general behaviour of both mousebirds is much the same as for the Redfaced Mousebird (following pages) except that neither flies in compact groups as does the Redfaced; they tend to follow one another in a straggling procession. Otherwise their food requirements and manner of feeding are similar.

OTHER NAMES: SPECKLED MOUSEBIRD
SPECKLED COLY
Gevlekte Muisvoël
Colius striatus

VOICE
Both mousebirds call while feeding, the Whitebacked a musical 'swee, weewit' and the Speckled a harsh 'zik, zik'.

Mousebirds often rest or feed while hanging below a branch. Here a Whitebacked Mousebird hangs by one foot while feeding on ripe guavas at a feeding station.

A POPULATION CHANGE

During 1962 Whitebacked Mousebirds arrived for the first time (according to available records) in the Johannesburg region, and breeding was recorded. For several years they prospered and became familiar about parks and gardens. Then, during the late 1970s, one or two Speckled Mousebirds were also seen for the first time, and by the mid 1980s they had become very common throughout the Witwatersrand. As the Speckled increased in numbers the Whitebacked Mousebirds decreased until, by 1986, they had disappeared from the region. It appears that the Whitebacked Mousebird is unable to compete with the bolder, more numerous Speckled Mousebird, although the Redfaced Mousebird is able to do so.

A Whitebacked Mousebird on its nest.

NESTING

The Whitebacked Mousebird builds a neat, bowl-shaped nest lined with plant-wool and placed in a bush. Two to four eggs are usually laid.

The nest of the Speckled Mousebird is untidy when compared to that of the Whitebacked, but is otherwise similar. In both the two to four eggs are incubated for up to 15 days and the chicks fledge at about ten days, climbing about the tree until able to fly.

The eggs of both mousebirds are white or creamy-white with a rough texture. They vary between a length of 16,3 mm and 24,2 mm.

A group of Speckled Mousebirds at the bird table.

IN THE GARDEN

Whitebacked Mousebirds will come readily to bird tables for soft fruits. In the garden they are wary feeders and do little harm. Speckled Mousebirds are bold and voracious feeders, often being the first to arrive at a bird table in flocks of up to 15 and demolishing any fruit with great rapidity. In some regions they are especially attracted to pawpaw and apples, whereas in other regions they have been known to stay away from bird tables in spite of a plentiful supply of these fruits. In the garden they are great pests, devouring young growing fruits long before they have ripened, and will eat peas, seedlings and certain succulent plants.

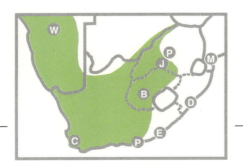

The distribution of these two mousebirds is mutually exclusive, the Whitebacked being mostly westerly and the Speckled easterly.

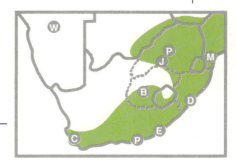

Redfaced Mousebird

NATIONAL NUMBER 426

OTHER NAMES
REDFACED COLY
Rooiwangmuisvoël
Colius indicus

VOICE
The Redfaced Mousebird makes a melodious, descending 'chui-chui-chui', both while feeding and in flight.

Of our three mousebirds the Redfaced is probably the most common and certainly the most widespread. It is distinct in having red facial skin surrounding the eyes and extending onto the upper bill. In common with the other mousebirds, it has red feet, a long, stiff tail and soft, elongated head feathers which form a crest. The sexes are alike.

The Redfaced Mousebird occurs in flocks of about ten birds which feed on berries, fruit and buds, scrambling about the tree with remarkable agility. The flock flies as a compact group and, on arrival at the next tree, crash into the foliage and then remain motionless momentarily prior to feeding again.

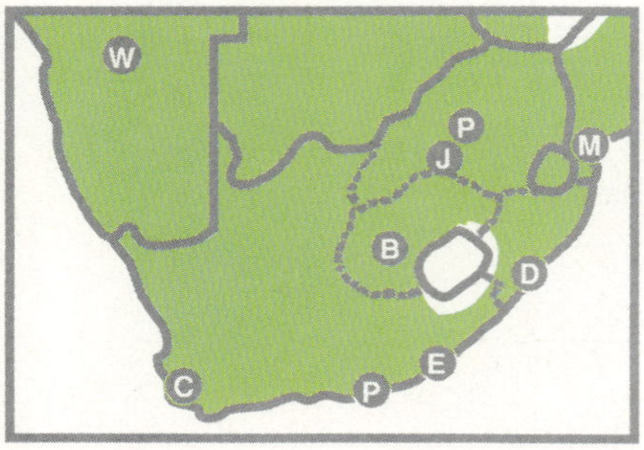

The Redfaced Mousebird is found throughout the country in bushveld, riverine bush and urban regions.

A Redfaced Mousebird on its nest in a Protea bush; note that string has been used in the nest construction.

NESTING
A softly lined, untidy bowl of rootlets and soft twigs is placed within the foliage of a medium-sized tree. The birds are sensitive to disturbance during the early stages and may destroy both nest and eggs. Two to four eggs are normally laid and hatch after about 14 days. The chicks leave the nest at 15 days, before they are able to fly, and continue their development while climbing about in the branches, their parents feeding them until they are able to forage with the main flock.

The egg colour of the Redfaced Mousebird varies between pure white and creamy, sparsely speckled and scrolled with reddish-brown. They measure on average 21 mm in length.

Mousebirds tame easily and become charming pets, being one of the few birds that will tolerate human handling.

IN THE GARDEN
This mousebird is not easily attracted to bird tables, but may succumb to regular offerings of pawpaw. After a while the birds become bolder and arrive at the bird table in numbers of up to ten. It has a particular liking for ripe figs and may become a temporary nuisance if these are not netted. Otherwise it seldom attacks garden fruits, being more partial to berries such as those of the *Cotoneaster* bush.

Giant Kingfisher

NATIONAL NUMBER 429

OTHER NAMES
Reuse Visvanger
Ceryle maxima

This, the largest of our kingfishers, has become a frequent visitor to garden fish ponds in many parts of the country, especially where properties border quiet rivers. It has a voracious appetite and will often attempt to seize a fish too large for it to handle. On the other hand on rivers it consumes many crabs as well as fish. Unmistakable, with dark plumage, large crested head and massive bill; the male with a chestnut breast, the female a chestnut belly.

VOICE
The Giant Kingfisher generally announces its presence with its loud call, a raucous, agitated 'kek-kek-kek-kek-kek' given either in flight or while perched.

The bird on the left has caught a goldfish from a garden pond. If kingfishers over-fish a garden pond then the water should be covered with a soft plant net for a few weeks; this should be staked a few centimetres above the surface. Photo: Nico Myburgh.

This Giant Kingfisher has caught a small river crab, a food item to which this species is particularly partial. Photo: Peter Steyn.

NESTING
The Giant Kingfisher breeds August–January and excavates a tunnel a metre or more in length in a river bank. A chamber is excavated at the far end in which three to five eggs are laid. Incubation and nestling times have not been recorded but it is known that both parents feed the young while they are in the nest and for some time after fledging.

The Giant Kingfisher lays rounded, white eggs measuring on average 45,5 mm in length.

IN THE GARDEN
The only way in which this large kingfisher can be attracted to the garden is by providing a well-stocked fish pond with a convenient perch from which it can operate. It will take fish, crabs and frogs, which are beaten into immobility before being swallowed. It will not eat dead fish or visit a bird table for alternative foods. Often the Giant Kingfisher will seize a fish too large to be swallowed immediately. The bird then swallows the fish in stages with the tail protruding from its beak. This may take as long as 20 minutes.

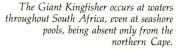

The Giant Kingfisher occurs at waters throughout South Africa, even at seashore pools, being absent only from the northern Cape.

55

Malachite Kingfisher

NATIONAL NUMBER 431

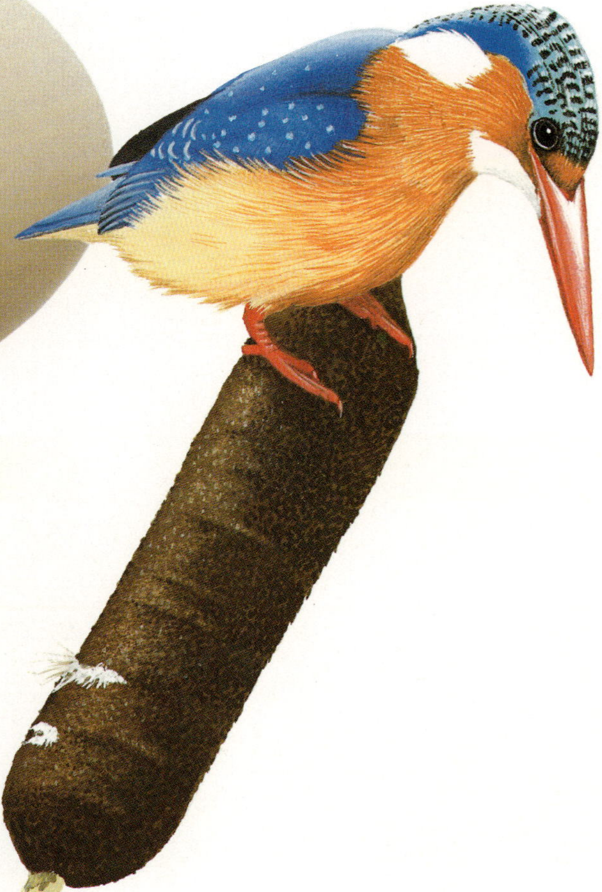

OTHER NAMES
Kuifkopvisvanger
Alcedo cristata

This Malachite Kingfisher has a black bill which indicates an immature bird; note that the adult, as shown above, has a red bill.

This jewel-like little bird has become a frequent visitor to garden fish ponds in many parts of the country. Since it arrives silently, and because of its small size, it is frequently overlooked and may take many small fish before departing. It perches on foliage close to the water and plunge-dives for its prey before setting off like an arrow for the next fish pond. The sexes are alike.

The Malachite Kingfisher can be found on inland waters throughout the country except for the drier regions of the western and northern Cape. It prefers still waters and will frequent even temporary rain pools.

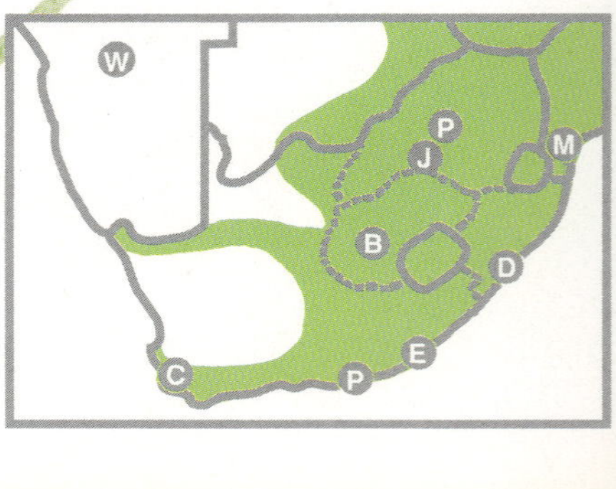

VOICE
This is normally a silent bird but, if flushed, will fly off uttering a shrill 'peep-peep'.

NESTING
In common with the Giant Kingfisher (previous pages) the Malachite excavates a tunnel in a bank with a nest-chamber at the far end, the tunnel being up to a metre in length. Three to five eggs are laid but the incubation and nestling times are unknown. The nest-chamber becomes littered with fish bones and insect remains.

The glossy white eggs of the Malachite Kingfisher have an average length of 18,7 mm.

IN THE GARDEN
This kingfisher eats small fish, tadpoles, frogs and dragonflies and can only be attracted by a garden pond. The introduction of small indigenous fish will prove less costly than slow-breeding goldfish. It is a good idea to provide a perch in the pond for the Malachite Kingfisher. This can take the form of a rock as shown above or a stick as seen on the right. The use of a rock has a real advantage for kingfisher-watchers in that the kingfisher will return to it with its catch and proceed to immobilise it by beating it on the rock before swallowing.

Hoopoe

NATIONAL NUMBER 451

OTHER NAMES
Hoephoep
Upupa epops

This dove-sized cinnamon-brown bird with its conspicuous erectile crest and curved bill is well known and unmistakable, being equally at home in the bushveld or the average garden. Its flight is low and undulating with a butterfly-like quality, an impression created by its black and white wing-barring.

The Hoopoe feeds mostly on insects and their larvae or worms obtained by probing in the ground with its bill, but it will also eat small lizards and small snakes when the opportunity occurs. The sexes are similar, the female being a little duller, while the juvenile is a small, scruffy version of the female.

VOICE
The call of the Hoopoe is a mellow sounding 'hoop hoop hoop'; it will also make a 'zweee' sound when alarmed. Young birds call 'sweet sweet'.

The Hoopoe occurs throughout the country and has become a familiar bird in many well-wooded urban areas.

A Hoopoe hovers as it feeds its chicks in a natural tree cavity. Photo: Peter Steyn.

NESTING

The Hoopoe nests in a cavity in a wall, old tree, termite mound or beneath the eaves of a house, sometimes using the same nest in successive years. The nest is unlined and the two to six eggs are incubated by the female for 17 days. The chicks remain in the nest for up to 32 days and are fed by both parents. The nest assumes a strong musky odour.

Normally the Hoopoe carries its crest depressed, as seen in this picture of a bird and its nest. The crest is raised mostly when landing or when the bird is alarmed.

When laid the Hoopoe's eggs are bluish-white or olive-green, but during incubation they fade to brownish or greyish in colour. They average 25 mm in length.

IN THE GARDEN

While the Hoopoe is a common garden bird in most regions it is difficult to attract to bird tables. Where bone-meal is regularly provided it is possible that the Hoopoe will take to picking up the fallen scraps and may, thereafter, take it directly from the table.

The Hoopoe will accept an artificial nest box of the correct dimensions, a horizontally placed pipe or hollow log being ideal. The inside dimensions should measure approximately 45–60 cm × 20 cm. One end should be well sealed and the opening at the opposite end reduced to a narrow vertical slit not more than 8 cm wide × 10 cm deep (the Hoopoe likes to squeeze through the entrance gap). The pipe or log should be securely fixed to a tree or a high wall well before the start of spring.

Redbilled Woodhoopoe

NATIONAL NUMBER 452

OTHER NAMES
REDBILLED HOOPOE
Gewone Kakelaar; Rooibekkakelaar
Phoeniculus purpureus

The Redbilled Woodhoopoe is found in woodland and well-wooded suburbia throughout the Transvaal and much of Natal and the eastern coastal region to beyond Port Elizabeth.

Whereas the Redbilled Woodhoopoe appears blackish in poor light it really is a very colourful bird with its iridescent greenish and purple plumage, plus red bill and feet. The male is larger than the female and they are usually seen in groups of up to a dozen birds, including black-billed immatures. Somewhat nomadic by day, the flock feeds by flying in straggling procession from tree to tree where each individual probes beneath the bark for insects, spiders and lizards. At night the flock retires to a regularly used roost.

A male Redbilled Woodhoopoe bringing food to nestlings in a nest-log tied to a floodlight pole. The nest had previously been used by Cardinal Woodpeckers.

VOICE
The call of the Redbilled Woodhoopoe is a loud cackling resembling high-pitched, hysterical laughter started by one bird and taken up by the entire flock. While calling the birds may gather together and all perform exaggerated bowing movements, their heads and tails alternately rising and falling.

NESTING
The Redbilled Woodhoopoe may breed in any month of the year but prefers the period July–November, during which time it may produce two broods. Usually a natural tree cavity is chosen, often the one in which the bird roosts, but the nests of woodpeckers and barbets are also used, as are nest-boxes. Two to five (usually three) eggs are laid and incubated by the female for about 18 days. During this time she is fed by one or more males. The chicks are in the nest for up to 30 days and are fed by their parents and by other members of the flock.

The dull, greenish-blue eggs of the Redbilled Woodhoopoe are pitted with numerous fine white pores. They average 24,8 mm in length.

Redbilled Woodhoopoes may sometimes be seen visiting the nests of sparrows and weavers, whether occupied or old, in search of fly grubs that often infest dirty nests. While examining occupied nests Woodhoopoes may evict any eggs or small chicks that they encounter. Sparrows and weavers are therefore usually hostile to their presence.

IN THE GARDEN
This woodhoopoe will feed at bird tables, especially during winter, to eat mealie pap or bone-meal, picking up small morsels in the tip of its bill and swallowing it with a toss of its head. It will eat fruit occasionally, especially ripe figs. It can also be encouraged to breed in the garden by the presence of a nest-log.

Blackcollared Barbet

NATIONAL NUMBER 464

OTHER NAMES
TOO-PUDDLEY
Rooikophoutkapper
Lybius torquatus

The Blackcollared Barbet is slightly smaller than the Crested Barbet and is highly distinctive with its crimson head and neck, black nape and collar and yellowish underparts. Usually in pairs or small groups, this barbet occurs commonly in wooded suburbs. On the ground it hops with tail raised. The sexes are alike.

VOICE
The call is a duet, and one not easily forgotten. It starts with a low 'kurr, kurr' then changes to a fast repetition of 'too-puddley, too-puddley . . .' accompanied by head-bobbing and wing-raising, the first bird calling 'too' and the second bird 'puddley'.

The question is often asked, 'Why is this bird not called the Redfronted Barbet?' In fact in ornithological terms a bird's 'front' is its forehead, and several other barbets also have red fronts. In this species the red colouring also extends to its ear coverts, face and throat, yet does not cover its entire head. Therefore the name Blackcollared Barbet is the most correct, if not the most descriptive.

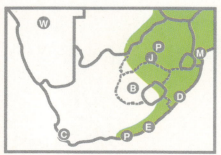

The Blackcollared Barbet ranges northwards along the coast from Port Elizabeth and over much of Natal, the Transvaal and northern Free State, preferring well-wooded regions.

NESTING

Breeding takes place mostly September–November and, in common with other barbets, the Blackcollared bores a hole in a tree for nesting purposes, preferring a dead branch in a softwood tree (see opposite page). The nest-chamber is about 250 mm below the entrance hole and two to five eggs are laid, more usually three. The incubation period is 14–19 days and the nestling period up to 35 days with both parents and often other adults feeding the nestlings. Up to four broods may be raised in a season.

All barbets have a liking for ripe figs, and the Blackcollared is no exception. Growing figs can best be covered with old stockings for protection, leaving a few for the birds.

In common with most hole-nesting birds the Blackcollared Barbet lays white eggs. They average 24,3 mm in length.

The Blackcollared Barbet responds readily to a supply of soft fruits on the bird table.

IN THE GARDEN

The Blackcollared Barbet is probably heard more than seen but will certainly frequent bird tables well stocked with fruit during winter, although it is less inclined to take mealie pap or dog food. They will also breed in artificial nest-logs or nest-boxes provided that the entrance hole in the box is no larger than 50 mm in diameter. In nest-logs they should be allowed to make their own entrance: they will usually ignore a ready-made hole.

Crested Barbet
NATIONAL NUMBER 473

OTHER NAMES
Kuifkophoutkapper
Trachyphonus vaillantii

VOICE
The call of the Crested Barbet can be heard at any time of the year; a rather monotonous trilling purr resembling the muffled bell of an alarm clock 'trrrrrrrrrrr . . .'. The call usually lasts about 30 seconds and may be frequently repeated, becoming louder and shriller if the bird is agitated by the sight of a cat or dog.

A striking, medium-sized bird with crested head and heavy yellow bill, highly colourful in plumage of yellow, black, red and white. The Crested Barbet is arguably our most colourful garden bird, being common and confiding in urban areas of the Transvaal and Natal. It is found in wooded gardens and often perches conspicuously when calling. On the ground it hops with an upright gait, the tail and crest held raised. The sexes are closely similar.

At the bird table the Crested Barbet will eat fruit, mealie pap, bone-meal, bread and dog food.

NESTING

The Crested Barbet breeds August–February. In common with the woodpeckers, to which it is related, it nests in a hole bored into a tree trunk or branch, the exotic soft-wood willow being particularly favoured. Three eggs are normally laid in the nest-chamber, which is about 350 mm below the entrance, and are incubated for 17 days. The nestling period is 27–30 days with both parents feeding the chicks. Often two, three or even four broods may be raised in a season.

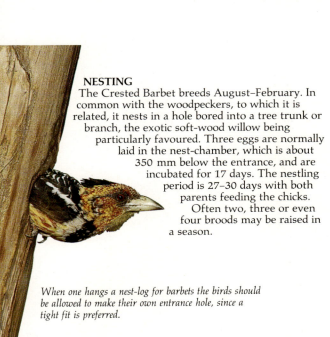

When one hangs a nest-log for barbets the birds should be allowed to make their own entrance hole, since a tight fit is preferred.

The white eggs of the Crested Barbet average 28 mm in length.

IN THE GARDEN

The Crested Barbet feeds on insects and fruit, and will therefore readily respond to a supply of fruit on the bird table, especially pawpaw (or pawpaw skins), apples and pears. In addition it will also eat mealie pap, mixed dog food and bone-meal.
It may be encouraged to nest in the garden if suitable nest-logs, or nest-boxes, are supplied: see section on nest-logs.

The apple on this pole is not defying gravity but has been deliberately nailed in position to prevent the Crested Barbet from knocking it to the ground or carrying it away.

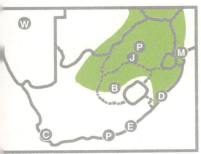

The Crested Barbet is found in much of Natal, throughout the Transvaal and in the northern Cape, always in well-wooded regions, including riverine bush.

Cape Wagtail

NATIONAL NUMBER 713

OTHER NAMES
WILLIE WAGTAIL
Gewone Kwikkie
Motacilla capensis

This popular and friendly little bird is a common garden visitor and well known for its ever-bobbing tail and confiding nature. It emits cheerful whistles as it struts about lawns searching for insects or hovers over swimming pools to pluck insects from the surface, and shows little fear even of domestic animals. Normally the Cape Wagtail is seen in pairs, the sexes being identical.

VOICE
The normal call is a pleasant 'cheep' or 'tsee-eep' uttered while walking or in flight.

Here a pair of Cape Wagtails have their nest in a garden tree. Photo: Peter Steyn.

NESTING
The Cape Wagtail breeds at any time of the year but mostly during early summer. The nest is a bulky structure of rootlets, grasses and plant stems with a neat central cup lined with hair or plant fibres and placed in any convenient niche. In a garden situation this can be in a wall cavity, tree stump, hanging flower pot, shed, gutter, etc. Three eggs are usually laid and incubated by both sexes for 14 days. The nestling period is about 14 days with both parents feeding the chicks.

The eggs of the Cape Wagtail are putty coloured, mottled brownish overall, their average length being 21 mm.

A Cape Wagtail attracted to a bird table by bone-meal.

IN THE GARDEN
In a natural environment the Cape Wagtail is a waterside bird, usually found on river banks or near damp vleis, and is therefore often attracted to garden ponds. Otherwise it will enter well-watered gardens in search of insects and can be attracted to the bird table with bone-meal, meat fat or mince.

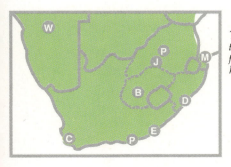
The Cape Wagtail occurs throughout the country, favouring waterside or garden habitats.

Pied Crow

NATIONAL NUMBER 548

OTHER NAMES
Witborskraai
Corvus albus

This common crow is told by its striking pied plumage, the only local crow with a white breast, the sexes and young birds all being alike. Common and widespread throughout most of the country, it is found singly or in small foraging parties. It is entirely omnivorous and opportunistic in its feeding habits, taking anything edible from insects, small mammals, fish, frogs, carrion, grain, fruit and kitchen scraps. It is a frequent visitor to refuse dumps where it is occasionally seen in large flocks.

VOICE
The normal call of the Pied Crow is a harsh 'kwaaak' but at times it also makes a strange bubbling 'kwallop kwallop . . .'.

The Pied Crow is found virtually throughout the country, preferring the less wooded regions. It avoids evergreen forests.

NESTING
This crow normally breeds in early summer, building a large and deep cup-shaped nest of twigs and sticks and lined with hair, roots or vegetable matter, which is placed in a high tree (often a conifer) or telephone pole. Four to five eggs are laid and incubated for about 18 days mostly by the female. Both parents feed the chicks during their 33–45 day nestling period.

Young, well-grown Pied Crows in their nest waiting to be fed by their parents.

The eggs of the Pied Crow have a variable ground colour of pale bluish-green or pale khaki, and are well spotted and mottled with brown. They average 45 mm in length.

IN THE GARDEN
The Pied Crow is common in many urban areas, especially in country towns and the outlying suburbs of cities. It frequents school playing fields and gardens provided they are not too wooded. In gardens it normally feeds on worms, crickets and caterpillars in lawns but, being an opportunistic species, it will certainly visit the bird table once it has identified it as a food source, and may consequently become a regular visitor.

Blackeyed Bulbul and Cape Bulbul

NATIONAL NUMBERS RESPECTIVELY 568 AND 566

OTHER NAMES: BLACKEYED BULBUL
TOPPIE; TIPTOL
Swartoogtiptol
Pycnonotus barbatus

These common, lively species with their tufted heads and yellow vents are well adapted to a human environment, preferring gardens with fruit-bearing trees and bushes. Their cheerful calls and excited chattering serve to make their presence known. At bird tables with a regular supply of fruits they become very tame and confiding. The sexes are alike.

The spectacled appearance of the Cape Bulbul is highly diagnostic. Photo: Peter Steyn.

OTHER NAMES: CAPE BULBUL
TOPPIE
Kaapse Tiptol
Pycnonotus capensis

VOICE
The call of the Blackeyed Bulbul is a series of lively, liquid notes resembling the words 'Wake up, Gregory' or 'come back to Calcutta', although sometimes only a part of the phrase is uttered. It also makes a twittering sound when excited, often several birds in unison, and makes a continuous 'chit, chit, chit . . .' prior to roosting. The Cape Bulbul has a similar repertoire to the Blackeyed but the voice is rather higher pitched, less mellow.

NESTING
These bulbuls breed in summer, especially in October, and build a shallow, rather flimsy cup nest using rootlets, hair and fine grasses. It is placed on an outer branch of a small tree. Three eggs are normally laid. In the Blackeyed Bulbul the eggs are incubated for 12–14 days by the female who is fed by the male at this time. The nestings are fed by both parents for about 12 days and for some days after fledging.

Nothing is known about the incubation and nestling period of the Cape Bulbul but it probably follows closely that of the Blackeyed Bulbul.

A Blackeyed Bulbul at its flimsy nest.

The eggs of the Blackeyed Bulbul (left) and the Cape Bulbul (right) are similar, having a ground colour of pinkish-white with a dense speckling of reddish and purple-grey. In both species the eggs average 23,5 mm in length.

IN THE GARDEN
Both bulbuls feed on nectar, fruit, berries and insects and are easily attracted to bird tables. Their favourite fruits are apples and pawpaws but almost any soft fruit will attract them. They will also eat bone-meal.

The Blackeyed Bulbul ranges commonly over the eastern half of the country from Port Elizabeth northwards, while the Cape Bulbul is restricted to the southern Cape coastal belt where it is common in Cape Town and Port Elizabeth.

BLACKEYED BULBUL   CAPE BULBUL

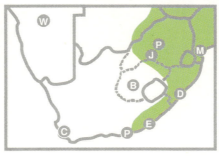
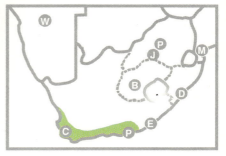

Kurrichane Thrush and Olive Thrush

NATIONAL NUMBERS RESPECTIVELY 576 AND 577

These two common thrushes are similar in appearance but, whereas the Kurrichane enters gardens only on a limited scale in scattered localities, the Olive Thrush has become a common garden bird in most urban areas. In both species the sexes are alike.

**OTHER NAMES:
KURRICHANE THRUSH**
Rooibeklyster
Turdus libonyana

NOTE *The name Kurrichane (pronounced 'Kurri-cha-nie') is derived from a town previously of that name in the western Transvaal, now known as Zeerust.*

**OTHER NAMES:
OLIVE THRUSH
CAPE THRUSH**
Olyflyster
Turdus olivaceus

The Kurrichane Thrush, normally a bird of woodland, differs from the Olive Thrush in having a pale eyebrow and more white on the throat, upon which the black markings form distinct stripes on either side. The belly is also white, and sometimes (depending on locality) the white extends forward along the central breast. The bill is orange.

VOICE
The Kurrichane Thrush has a loud and mellow song, a complicated series of trills and clear notes in short outbursts. Otherwise it calls 'peet-peeoo, peet-peeoo' on take-off or repeatedly at nightfall.

A Kurrichane Thrush at its nest and nestlings near Loskop Dam in the Transvaal.

The larger Olive Thrush is a bird of evergreen forests but has adapted freely to well-wooded suburbia. In this species the small white throat-patch is heavily speckled black, while the underparts are much duller than in the Kurrichane. This is particularly noticeable in birds of the Highveld regions. Elsewhere, especially in forests, the underparts are more richly coloured deep orange as illustrated. The bill is chrome-yellow.

VOICE
The Olive Thrush calls a thin 'wheet' when taking off and has a loud, mellow song 'trootee-trootee-trootee-trootee-trootee, treetrroo . . ' delivered in short outbursts and often for long periods before and after breeding.

An Olive Thrush at its nest. This picture, taken near Johannesburg, illustrates the dull colouring of the race.

This Olive Thrush's nest in a yellowwood tree is decorated with coloured string, red plastic and computer paper.

NESTING
Both thrushes breed September–January and build substantial, bowl-shaped nests in trees. Rootlets, twigs and grass are used in the construction, often interwoven with leaves, paper or discarded plastic. The interior is lined with mud and two or three eggs are laid. In both species the female incubates the eggs for 14 days, after which the nestlings are fed by both parents for a further 14–16 days.

IN THE GARDEN
Both thrushes feed on insects, spiders, worms, snails, small reptiles and fruit and can therefore easily be attracted to the bird table with bone-meal, apples, dog food and mealie pap. In gardens with fish ponds the Olive Thrush has been known to catch and eat small fish. More usually it catches earthworms in lawns, peering closely with head turned sideways, before plunging its beak into the ground.

The Kurrichane Thrush lays pale bluish-green eggs finely mottled with reddish-brown (right), while those of the Olive Thrush (left) are bright blue, well blotched with red-brown and slate. Those of the Kurrichane average 26,5 mm and those of the Olive Thrush 29,3 mm in length.

The Kurrichane Thrush occurs in bushveld and woodland regions of Natal and the Transvaal, entering gardens on the fringes of towns.

The Olive Thrush, outside of evergreen forests, ranges widely as a garden bird. It is also seen commonly in urban parks.

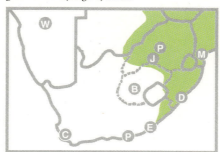 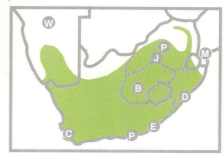

Natal Robin

NATIONAL NUMBER 600

OTHER NAMES
REDCAPPED ROBIN
Nataljanfrederik
Cossypha natalensis

In the Natal Robin the bluish-grey upperparts contrast sharply with the orange underparts, face and upper tail-coverts. The top of the head and the nape are brownish. A typical robin, alert and quick in its actions, the tail being frequently jerked upwards and fanned to expose the orange underfeathers. The sexes are alike. This robin is even more confined to dense bush and thickets than the Cape Robin (following pages) and is more easily seen when it is most active in the early mornings and evenings.

The Natal Robin has greyish upperparts in contrast to most others of the family.

VOICE
A fine songster and an extremely good mimic, and as such has a wide repertoire ranging from the calls of other birds to the whistling of herdmen. Its call note is a monotonous, frog-like 'creep-croop' repeated for long periods.

NESTING
The breeding period is September–January. The cup-shaped nest, constructed of dead leaves and twigs and lined with fibrous materials, is frequently placed in a cavity in an old tree stump, a crevice in a bank or in dense hanging vegetation. Two or three eggs are laid and incubated by the female for 15 days. The nestlings are fed by both parents for up to 17 days. This robin is often parasitised by the Redchested Cuckoo.

IN THE GARDEN
This secretive robin ventures into old, well-established gardens and parks in coastal towns and cities such as Durban and its suburbs. It is insectivorous and frugivorous and can probably be enticed to a bird table with offerings of bone-meal and pawpaw provided that the table is close to cover.

The eggs of the Natal Robin may be chocolate-brown or olive-green in colour. The average egg length is 22,5 mm.

The rufous crown of the Natal Robin gives rise to its alternative name of Redcapped Robin.

The distribution of the Natal Robin is mainly easterly from East London northwards. It is found in thickets in coastal bush, evergreen forests and valley bush where it is active in the lower stratum.

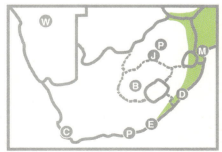

Cape Robin
NATIONAL NUMBER 601

OTHER NAMES
Gewone Janfrederik
Cossypha caffra

The Cape Robin frequents gardens within the shelter of dense bushes and undergrowth, coming onto lawns in search of insects in the early mornings and evenings. It hops and feeds with a sprightly action, making frequent short flights in which the tail is raised and spread on landing. Usually shy and quick to return to cover, it will nevertheless bathe in the spray of a garden sprinkler, and tolerate a close approach provided no sudden movements are made. The sexes are alike; young birds are duller and spotted above and below.

VOICE
The Cape Robin has a low, harsh alarm call 'waa, waa-deedaa'. Its song is a pleasant repertoire of repeated phrases, each starting on the same note 'teeu teedle-dee, teeu teedle weedle, teeu teetoo, teeu teetoo tiddle . . .'. This is heard mostly early mornings, often before dawn, and at last light.

NESTING
The breeding season of the Cape Robin extends from June–January in the winter rainfall region and from September–January in the summer rainfall region. The nest is placed in some low bush, in flood debris on a river bank, in a wall creeper, wall crevice or on the ground. The nest itself is a mass of rootlets, grass, twigs, etc. with a neat central cup lined with hair or plant fibres in which two or three eggs are laid. The female incubates the eggs for 14–19 days after which the nestlings are fed by both parents for about 16 days.

The eggs of the Cape Robin are usually pale pinkish finely speckled all over with rust, this sometimes forming a zone around the broad end. The eggs average 23,5 mm in length.

ABOVE *A Cape Robin feeding its nestling in a silverleaf tree.*

BELOW *This Cape Robin's nest is placed in flood debris on a river bank, a favourite site for the species.*

IN THE GARDEN

This well-loved robin is not easily tempted onto the bird table but, being almost entirely insectivorous, it can be enticed with bone-meal (see photograph on far left). With patience and perseverence it will take small items of meat, cheese or mealworms from the hand. With encouragement it will enter the house and feed from the table. An old paint tin or flower pot placed firmly in a hedge, creeper or dense bush will often be accepted as a nest site.

The Cape Robin is found throughout the country except for the northern Cape and extreme northern Transvaal. Its normal habitat is evergreen forest edges, wooded kloofs, riverine bush and mountain scrub but it also occurs in most well-wooded urban areas.

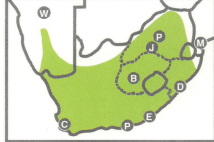

77

Migrant warblers

GARDEN WARBLER
NATIONAL NUMBER 619
Tuinsanger
Sylvia borin

The Garden Warbler has few distinctive markings, having grey-brown upperparts, greyish-white underparts and a rather short bill. It is highly secretive, always retiring to the interior of a dense bush from where it sings a quiet and prolonged warble of rapid notes 'trrootrroo-churr-prooee-chirpchirp zee-zee chirrup zeree zeree chirp prooee . . .' with only brief pauses. It also has a sharp 'chak-chak' call note.

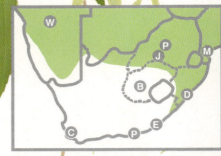

The Garden Warbler is found during the summer months throughout the eastern and northern regions of the country; it is absent from the western Cape and the dry interior.

The birds in these pictures are non-breeding migrants to southern Africa, coming annually from Europe, Scandinavia and Siberia. They arrive in South Africa from October onwards, spending our summer (their winter) in our bushveld, woodlands and gardens, mostly returning to the same location every year. Since they are very small, sombrely coloured and often secretive, they are generally overlooked, but once their distinctive songs are known and recognised they are found to be surprisingly numerous. They start returning to their northern hemisphere breeding grounds in March.

EUROPEAN MARSH WARBLER
NATIONAL NUMBER 633
Europese Rietsanger
Acrocephalus palustris

This species is olivaceous-brown above with a cinnamon wash on the white underparts; it has distinct pale eyebrows and pink legs. The European Marsh Warbler is also secretive, staying mostly in dense thickets from where it sings quietly for long periods, but it will show itself briefly from time to time. The song, in which it mimics other bird calls, is a rapid jumble of mellow notes 'peet-peet skree skree skree, chiree chiree, tuc tuc chirree, trrrr trrrr, swee swee . . .'. It also has a 'tuc' call note and a 'tcchhh' alarm call.

The European Marsh Warbler occurs during the summer months along the east coast to about Port Elizabeth, and throughout Natal, Zululand and the Transvaal.

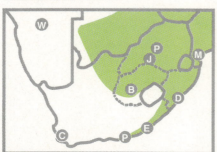

NOTE
Since these migrant warblers feed entirely on small insects it is not possible to attract them to a bird table.

The Willow Warbler will sometimes feed among weeds or on the ground as seen in this brown form. Photo: Nico Myburgh.

WILLOW WARBLER
NATIONAL NUMBER 643
Hofsanger
Phylloscopus trochilus

The Willow Warbler, one of the first migrants to arrive, can be seen almost anywhere in trees and bushes during summer, actively gleaning insects from the foliage, its presence often first revealed by its call or song. The Willow Warbler occurs in two major colour forms as illustrated: with an overall yellow wash or without it. In both colour forms the eyebrows are prominent, the legs pinkish and the tail-tip is distinctly notched. The song, heard mostly in early summer and in February, is a pleasant series of descending notes 'tee-tee-tee-tu-tu-twee-twee-sweetsweetsweetsweet' repeated about every six seconds. It also calls a soft 'foo-wee' while feeding.

The Willow Warbler occurs throughout summer over the entire country with the exception of the extreme western Cape.

Tawnyflanked Prinia and Blackchested Prinia

NATIONAL NUMBERS RESPECTIVELY 683 AND 685

Prinias are small brown warblers characterised by long tails which are frequently held erect. They occur in rank grass, shrubs and low bushes, often along watercourses and usually in small family groups. They feed on small insects and, in both species, the sexes are alike.

OTHER NAMES: TAWNYFLANKED PRINIA
Bruinsylangstertjie
Prinia subflava

VOICE
The Tawnyflanked Prinia is often located by its alarm call, a mewing 'sbeeee, sbeeee' which may be taken up by several birds in a party. The call of both prinias is 'chip-chip-chip-chip-chip . . .' or 'zrrrrt-zrrrrt-zrrrrt'.

OTHER NAMES: BLACKCHESTED PRINIA
Swartbandlangstertjie
Prinia flavicans

NESTING

During October–March both species build an oval ball of woven grass or reed strips with an entrance on one upper side. It is lined with fine grasses or plant down and slung between grass blades, weed stems or in small bushes often with the surrounding foliage interwoven to form a roof. Three to four eggs are laid and incubated for 12–14 days by both sexes; the nestling period is between 12 and 15 days.

A Tawnyflanked Prinia at its nest; note how leaves have been incorporated into the structure.

Prinia nests are sometimes parasitised by the Cuckoo Finch (also known as the Parasitic Weaver). Here a Blackchested Prinia is seen feeding its foster-chick.

IN THE GARDEN

Both prinias may be common garden residents within the regions in which they occur. They subsist almost entirely on small insects and some nectar, and will soon become regular bird table visitors if oranges and bone-meal are available.

The colouring of the eggs of the prinias varies between individual females. On the left is a selection of those of the Tawnyflanked Prinia, and on the right those of the Blackchested. Both species lay eggs averaging 16 mm in length.

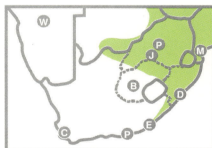

The distribution of the Tawnyflanked Prinia ranges along the east coast north from East London and westwards over most of the Transvaal.

The Blackchested Prinia has a westerly distribution, being mostly absent from Lowveld regions.

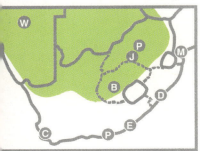

A Blackchested Prinia in winter plumage at the bird table; note the yellow wash on the underparts and the faded chest-band.

Fiscal Flycatcher

NATIONAL NUMBER 698

OTHER NAMES
Fiskaalvlieëvanger
Sigelus silens

This bird is often mistaken for the Fiscal Shrike (page 86), their plumage patterns, and even their behaviour, being superficially similar. However, note that the white wing-bar does not reach the shoulder in this species, whereas in the shrike it does. Also, the Fiscal Flycatcher is lighter in build and has a slender bill, not hooked as in the shrike. The female and immature birds are duller, being brownish above and dull white below, while newly fledged young are spotted above and below. The Fiscal Flycatcher, which is only found in South Africa, is commonly seen in pairs. It perches on a garden tree or fence from where it drops to the ground to seize an insect, often returning to the same perch to eat it.

The Fiscal Flycatcher is found throughout South Africa except in the extreme western and northern areas. In addition to parks and gardens it frequents a wide range of bushy habitats including those in semi-arid regions.

A male Fiscal Flycatcher attracted to the bird table by bone-meal. This individual carries an aluminium ring on its leg, placed there by members of the Southern African Ornithological Society. Such rings are numbered and serve to record the bird's longevity and movements in the event of its being recaptured later or recovered after death.

VOICE
The Fiscal Flycatcher has a wheezy, sibilant voice. The song is 'swee-swee-ur, trree trip trree, see sip seee, trrrr trip seee . . .' and similar sounds often in a prolonged and jumbled sequence.

NESTING
This flycatcher breeds mainly September–November, building a rather untidy bowl-shaped nest of twigs, grasses and rootlets which is placed in the fork of a tree. Usually three eggs are laid and incubated mainly by the female who is fed by the male for the 15 days of incubation, both sexes feeding the young in the nest and after fledging.

The eggs of the Fiscal Flycatcher are pale blue-green heavily mottled with reddish-brown, the mottling sometimes concentrated around the broad end. The eggs average 21 mm in length.

IN THE GARDEN
The Fiscal Flycatcher is a fairly common garden bird in most towns but is absent from the Natal coastal region during the summer months. It is mainly insectivorous but will eat some fruit. At the bird table it can be attracted by bone-meal.

Fiscal Flycatchers become remarkably tame in the garden, and will often be on hand to seize an insect when the earth is being turned.

Paradise Flycatcher

NATIONAL NUMBER 710

OTHER NAMES
Paradysvlieëvanger
Terpsiphone viridis

This graceful flycatcher makes its appearance in our gardens from about mid-October and departs again in March. The male with its long tail is quite unmistakable while the female, which is occasionally seen with a short tail-shaft, is also easily identified by its unique colouring. A highly active and vocal species, the Paradise Flycatcher frequents parks and gardens with large trees.

VOICE
The song is a pleasant, rippling 'wee-te-tiddly, wit-wit' with variations. Also calls frequently, a raspy 'zwee-zwer'.

ABOVE *The tail of the male Paradise Flycatcher can vary in length from between 185 mm and 300 mm.*

BELOW *A female may occasionally be seen with the two central tail feathers elongated to about twice the normal female tail length.*

The Paradise Flycatcher is found in the coastal belt from Cape Town to Natal and in suitable habitat over most of the Free State and the entire Transvaal. In March they depart, mostly moving north-east to Mozambique, but some remain in the Kruger National Park throughout winter.

NESTING

Breeding occurs mainly October–January. The nest, as illustrated, is a neat cup built of fine bark fibres and rootlets bound with spider web and decorated with lichen. It may be placed on the slender outer branch of a tree, often over water, or in the fork of a sapling and not more than about two and a half metres above ground. Two to three eggs are laid and are incubated for 12–15 days by both sexes. The nestling period averages 12 days, both parents feeding the young during this time and for at least a week after they fledge.

The Paradise Flycatcher lays creamy-white or pinkish eggs, lightly spotted with red-brown and slate, mostly concentrated in a ring around the broad end. Their average length is 18,7 mm.

IN THE GARDEN

The Paradise Flycatcher frequents well-wooded gardens throughout its range, announcing its presence by its lively actions and rippling call. It is entirely insectivorous and has not been known to visit bird tables although it may well learn to do so in response to regular offerings of bone-meal.

Often the exact destinations of migratory birds after they have left South Africa are not known but, in the case of the Paradise Flycatcher, there exist two records of ringed birds being recovered in Mozambique. The first, ringed in Pietermaritzburg, was recovered at Vila Junqueiro while the second, ringed in Johannesburg, was found near Beira.

Fiscal Shrike
NATIONAL NUMBER 732

OTHER NAMES
JACK(IE) HANGER; BUTCHER BIRD
Fiskaallaksman
Lanius collaris

This well-known black and white bird, with its heavy-headed appearance and hooked beak, has a bad reputation from its habit of attacking small birds and impaling them on a fence or thorn. The bird illustrated is a female, the male lacks the russet flank colour; compare this with the Fiscal Flycatcher on page 82 and note how, in the shrike, the white wing-bar extends fully to the bird's shoulder. In spite of its bad reputation the Fiscal Shrike is a useful bird in the garden since it eats a wide variety of insects.

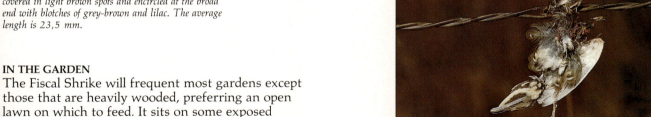

A pair of Fiscal Shrikes at their nest in an oak tree.

VOICE
The song of the Fiscal Shrike is a series of harsh, grating sounds mixed with some sweet notes and containing fragments of other birds' calls plus a frequently repeated 'gercha, gercha'.

The eggs of the Fiscal Shrike are cream or greenish, covered in light brown spots and encircled at the broad end with blotches of grey-brown and lilac. The average length is 23,5 mm.

NESTING
The Fiscal Shrike breeds mainly September–December, building a bulky cup-shaped nest of grass, twigs, leaves and other debris, which is placed in the fork of a tree. Three or four eggs are laid and these are incubated by the female for about 15 days while the male brings food. Thereafter both sexes feed the nestlings for up to 20 days and for some days after fledging.

The remains of a small bird impaled on a barbed wire fence by a Fiscal Shrike. Other prey items frequently impaled are grasshoppers, mice, lizards and frogs. These 'larders' are often forgotten by the shrike and the victim is left to rot.

IN THE GARDEN
The Fiscal Shrike will frequent most gardens except those that are heavily wooded, preferring an open lawn on which to feed. It sits on some exposed perch from where it flies to the ground to seize its prey. It can be attracted to the bird table with bone-meal or meat scraps and, with encouragement, will feed from the hand. However, since it does occasionally attack other small birds its constant presence may well dissuade others from visiting the bird table.

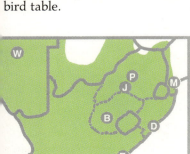

The Fiscal Shrike is widespread throughout the country in suitable habitat, preferring grassland with bushes, but is absent from forested regions.

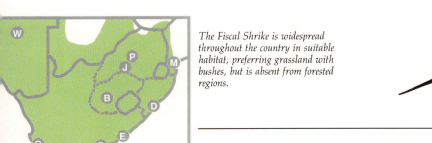

Southern Boubou
NATIONAL NUMBER 736

OTHER NAMES
BOUBOU SHRIKE
Suidelike Waterfiskaal
Laniarius ferrugineus

The Southern Boubou has a similar plumage pattern to the Fiscal Shrike (previous pages) but differs in having a pale rufous wash on the underparts, strongest on the flanks and belly, while the white wing-bar is broader. This shrike is secretive, staying mostly in dense bush and thickets where its presence is revealed by frequent calling. Spends much time on the ground and in the lower stratum of bushes, emerging only occasionally. Usually occurs in pairs, the female being duller on the upperparts.

VOICE
Pairs keep in touch by frequent duetting, of which there are many variations; typically the first bird calls a ringing 'ko-ko', the second replying 'kweeet', or 'boo-boo' answered by 'whee-oo', or a liquid 'phooweeol' answered by 'hueee' or 'churrrr'. The two calls are usually given in such rapid succession that they seem to be made by one bird. The alarm call is a harsh 'chaaa, chaaa'.

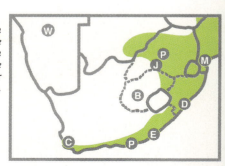

The Southern Boubou occurs in suitable habitat throughout the coastal regions from Cape Town northwards and over much of the Transvaal, avoiding the drier regions.

NESTING

The breeding season of the Southern Boubou is August–January in the winter rainfall region, mainly October–November in Natal and August–February in the Transvaal. This species constructs a shallow basin of roots, twigs and grasses which is bound with spider web, lined with fine grasses and well concealed in a dense bush or thick creeper, seldom higher than about two metres from the ground. Four eggs are usually laid, both sexes sharing in the 16 days of incubation. The nestling period is also 16 days, the chicks being dependent on their parents for about 54 days after fledging.

A Southern Boubou at its nest in a hibiscus hedge.

The eggs of the Southern Boubou may have a ground colour of pinkish-white, pale buff or greenish, sparingly marked with brown and pale lilac-grey encircling the broad end. They are on average 25 mm in length.

IN THE GARDEN

The Southern Boubou is well known in gardens with ample cover. Though some individuals become surprisingly bold, this shrike is usually first detected by the ringing call of a pair in duet. Being largely insectivorous it will come to bird tables for bone-meal and will also eat small amounts of fruit, mealie pap and dog food.

The Southern Boubou is a regular bather and will use a bird bath provided it is not too far from cover. Photo: Peter Steyn.

Puffback

NATIONAL NUMBER 740

OTHER NAMES
Sneeubal
Dryoscopus cubla

VOICE
Calls sharply while flying from tree to tree, a loud 'chick-weeu, chick-weeu' repeatedly; also calls a repetitive 'chick chick chick chick chick . . .'.

MALE

FEMALE

There are minor differences between the sexes in this small shrike, the female having a white forehead and eyebrow whereas the male has a black hood to below its red eyes. The vernacular names are derived from the male's habit of puffing its white rump plumes when courting; see illustration. The Puffback usually occurs in pairs and often in mixed bird parties. It frequents well-wooded gardens within its range but is otherwise found in woodland where it feeds in the tree canopy.

NESTING
Breeds mostly September–January, building a neat cup nest of grass and bark strips well bound with spider web and placed in the fork of a branch within a leafy tree. Two or three eggs are laid; both sexes share in the 13 days of incubation and feed the young.

MALE

The eggs of the Puffback are white, cream or pink, finely spotted with brown all over and with a dense zone of spots around the broad end. Their average length is 21,6 mm.

IN THE GARDEN
The Puffback is a common garden bird in many towns, but is usually restricted to gardens with large trees. There are no records of its visiting bird tables but it may well be tempted to do so when bone-meal is provided. Usually these birds prefer to forage in pairs in the tree canopies where they are easily detected because of the male's habit of calling repeatedly.

The Puffback occurs throughout the eastern regions of the country and into the Transvaal in mature woodland, riverine forests and on the edges of evergreen forests as far south as just beyond Port Elizabeth.

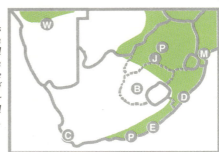

Bokmakierie

NATIONAL NUMBER 746

OTHER NAMES
Telophorus zeylonus

This distinctive and popular bush shrike is well known in residential areas for its striking plumage and song. It sings from the top of a tree, and can be heard throughout the year, but otherwise feeds on or near the ground where it runs rapidly in short bursts before stopping and standing erect briefly. It is often seen, normally in pairs, on lawns and in flower beds where it seeks insects and small reptiles. The sexes are alike but immature birds lack the black breast-band.

VOICE
The loud, ringing duets are very variable, the two birds calling almost simultaneously. The best known is that which gives rise to the species' name 'BOK-makiri' or 'kok-o-vik'. Other duets are 'pirrapee-pirrapoo', 'wit, wit-wit' with many regional variations.

NESTING
The Bokmakierie breeds July–October in the western Cape, July to March in the eastern Cape, September–March in Natal and mostly August–November in the Transvaal. The nest is a fairly large, compact cup of twigs, grasses and rootlets usually well concealed low down in a well-foliaged bush or tree. In a suburban environment it usually favours exotic, evergreen trees. Three to four eggs are laid and incubated for 14–17 days, probably by both sexes. Both sexes also feed the nestlings until they fledge at about 18 days.

A Bokmakierie brings food for its nestlings.

The Bokmakierie lays bluish or greenish eggs with a few rust spots and blotches. The average length is 25,6 mm.

IN THE GARDEN
This shrike favours lightly wooded gardens with lawns, but will avoid heavily wooded ones and will usually desert well-wooded suburbs entirely. It can be attracted to the bird table with bone-meal, meat fat or mixed dog food but otherwise feeds on insects picked up on the ground.

Since they are basically insectivorous Bokmakieries find a bird table provisioned with bone-meal irresistible.

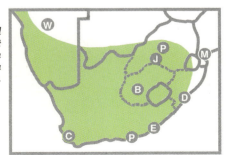

The Bokmakierie is widespread throughout the country except in the extreme northern Transvaal, and occurs in a very wide range of habitats.

European Starling and Indian Myna

NATIONAL NUMBERS RESPECTIVELY 757 AND 758

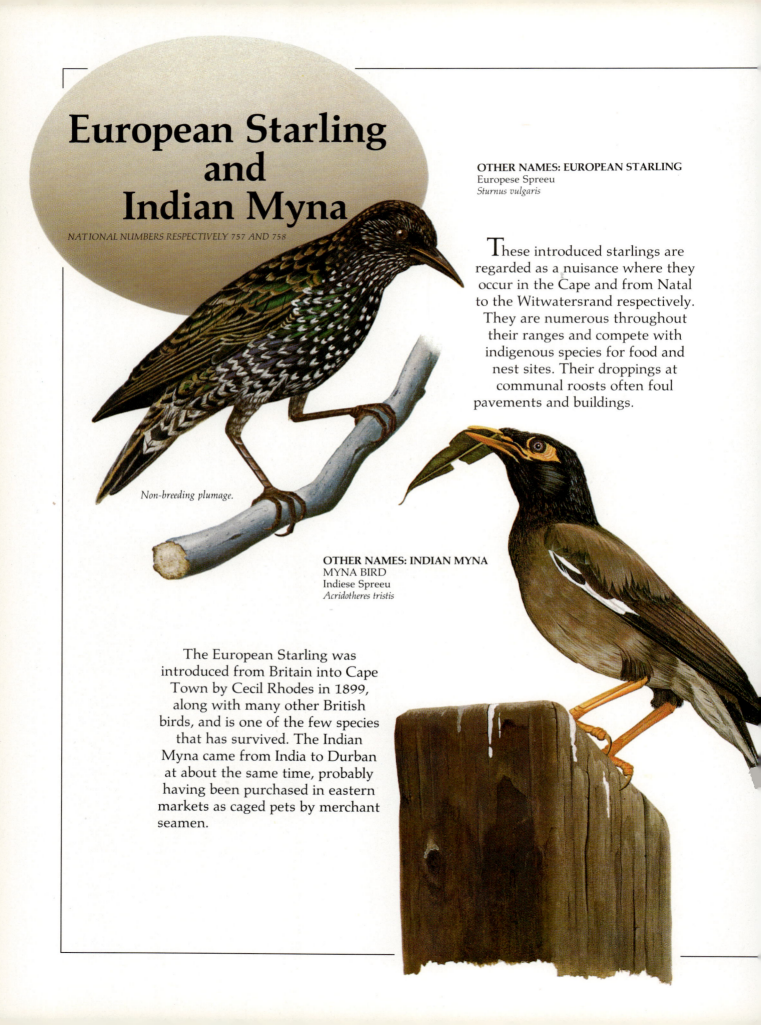

Non-breeding plumage.

OTHER NAMES: EUROPEAN STARLING
Europese Spreeu
Sturnus vulgaris

These introduced starlings are regarded as a nuisance where they occur in the Cape and from Natal to the Witwatersrand respectively. They are numerous throughout their ranges and compete with indigenous species for food and nest sites. Their droppings at communal roosts often foul pavements and buildings.

OTHER NAMES: INDIAN MYNA
MYNA BIRD
Indiese Spreeu
Acridotheres tristis

The European Starling was introduced from Britain into Cape Town by Cecil Rhodes in 1899, along with many other British birds, and is one of the few species that has survived. The Indian Myna came from India to Durban at about the same time, probably having been purchased in eastern markets as caged pets by merchant seamen.

VOICE

The European Starling utters a lively mixture of squeaks, whistles and croaking sounds, plus crude imitations of other bird calls. At communal roosts they make a considerable babbling.

The Indian Myna makes a variety of harsh croaks, squawks, creaks and whines, sometimes in a continuing sequence that is not altogether unpleasant. It has a harsh alarm note.

A European Starling in breeding plumage enjoying a bird bath. Photo: Peter Steyn.

NESTING

Both species breed September–December. The nests are loose bowls of twigs, grasses or pine needles — according to availability — plus paper, plastic and other rubbish placed in any convenient cavity. The European Starling lays three to six eggs which are incubated for 12 days by both sexes who also share the feeding of the chicks for the roughly 20 day nestling period. The Indian Myna lays four to five eggs but little is known about the incubation period; during the 25 day nestling period both parents and other helpers feed the chicks.

An Indian Myna at its nest in a ventilator pipe.

On the left is the pale blue egg of the European Starling and on the right the glossy blue egg of the Indian Myna. Both are on average 30 mm in length.

IN THE GARDEN

Both birds eat many insects in the garden but, at the bird table, they may become a nuisance since they are omnivorous and will devour anything available.

The European Starling has spread from Cape Town along the coast westwards to the Orange River mouth, and eastwards to southern Natal.

The Indian Myna occupies most of central Natal and has spread, or was introduced, to the Witwatersrand region and Pretoria.

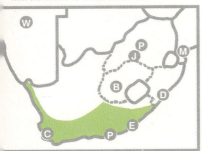
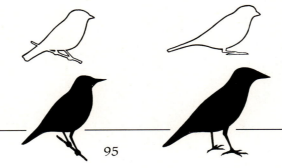
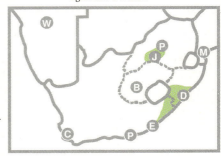

Plumcoloured Starling

NATIONAL NUMBER 761

OTHER NAMES
AMETHYST STARLING;
VIOLETBACKED STARLING
Witborsspreeu
Cinnyricinclus leucogaster

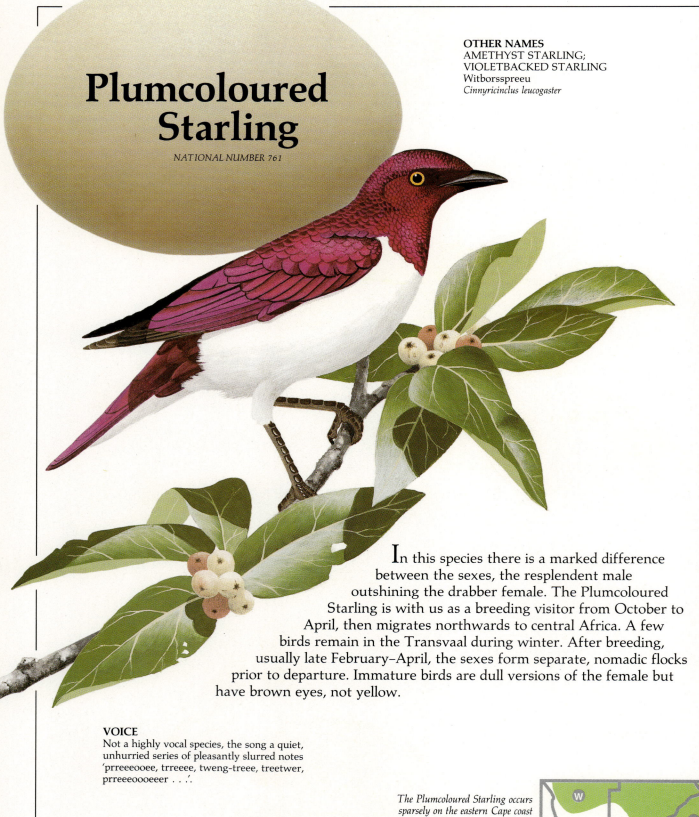

In this species there is a marked difference between the sexes, the resplendent male outshining the drabber female. The Plumcoloured Starling is with us as a breeding visitor from October to April, then migrates northwards to central Africa. A few birds remain in the Transvaal during winter. After breeding, usually late February–April, the sexes form separate, nomadic flocks prior to departure. Immature birds are dull versions of the female but have brown eyes, not yellow.

VOICE
Not a highly vocal species, the song a quiet, unhurried series of pleasantly slurred notes 'prreeeooee, trreeee, tweng-treee, treetwer, prreeeoooeeer . . .'.

The Plumcoloured Starling occurs sparsely on the eastern Cape coast and through most of Natal, Swaziland and the Transvaal. Its preferred habitat is woodland, riverine forest and well-wooded suburbia.

The female Plumcoloured Starling lacks the iridescent plumage of the male but is nevertheless strikingly marked.

NESTING

Breeding takes place October–February, the nest being placed in a ready-made tree-hole or metal fence post and consisting of a pad of grass and fresh leaves; fresh leaves are continually added throughout the incubation period. Three or four eggs are laid and these are incubated by the female for about 12 days. Both parents feed the chicks during the 21 day nestling period.

The eggs of the Plumcoloured Starling are pale bluish-green lightly spotted with reddish-brown and purple-grey. Their average length is 24,5 mm.

IN THE GARDEN

The Plumcoloured Starling is a shy species that seldom enters well-developed suburbs, preferring the quieter fringes of towns. It will visit secluded bird tables for soft fruit and bone-meal. A pair can be persuaded to nest in ready-made nest-logs and nest-boxes, or in metal fence posts provided the interior is filled with stones to within a distance of about 50 cm from the top.

A male Plumcoloured Starling perched on a fence post containing its nest. The ease and rapidity with which the birds enter and leave these post nests are remarkable.

Cape Glossy Starling

NATIONAL NUMBER 764

OTHER NAMES
GLOSSY STARLING
Kleinglansspreeu
Lamprotornis nitens

VOICE
The song is a pleasant 'trrr-treer-treer-cheer...', flocks becoming quite noisy. It also calls 'turr-treeu' on take-off.

This striking, iridescent blue-green starling with its yellow-orange eyes is a common bird in many towns and cities, although not in Cape Town or Durban. In East London a close relative, the smaller Blackbellied Glossy Starling, occurs with this bird. The Cape Glossy Starling usually occurs in pairs, the sexes being alike, but may gather in flocks at fruiting trees such as mulberries. In addition to fruit it also eats insects and nectar. It is a well-known sight at rest camps in the Kruger National Park, together with another close relative, the Greater Blue-eared Glossy Starling.

NESTING

The Cape Glossy Starling breeds mainly October–February in Natal and October–January, occasionally later, in the Transvaal. It nests in holes in trees, fence posts and in the eaves of buildings. The chosen cavity is lined with grass and leaves and two or three eggs are laid. The incubation period is not accurately known but is probably about 14 days, in common with other starlings of similar size. The nestling period is about 20 days with both parents feeding the chicks, helped by young birds from previous broods.

The pale blue eggs of the Cape Glossy Starling are lightly spotted with reddish-brown and measure, on average, 24,5 mm in length.

A Cape Glossy Starling has caught a small frog to feed to its nestlings, an example of the variety of insects and small animals that this bird is prepared to tackle.

IN THE GARDEN

Though rather shy the Cape Glossy Starling will frequent bird tables, especially during the winter months when natural food is less plentiful. It is partial to soft fruits, bone-meal, soft bread and mealie pap. At the onset of the breeding season, when nest holes are at a premium, the Cape Glossy Starling can be persuaded to nest in a ready-made nest-log or nest-box, since it is unable to excavate its own nest cavity.

The Cape Glossy Starling is absent from the coastal region of Cape Town to Port Elizabeth but is otherwise found throughout the country.

The Cape Glossy Starling (seen here) is predominantly glossy blue all over but can appear quite blackish in poor light, whereas its relative the Greater Blue-eared Glossy Starling is even more iridescent, being peacock-green on its wings, purple on its flanks and having a dark ear-patch. In the Kruger National Park the two species frequently feed together and give rise to much confusion.

Redwinged Starling

NATIONAL NUMBER 769

OTHER NAMES
Rooivlerkspreeu
Onychognathus morio

This large starling with its glossy black plumage and orange-red wing feathers is normally found in mountains and rocky kloofs but has become a regular garden bird in many localities, breeding and roosting in buildings. When not breeding it occurs in flocks and often becomes a pest on fruit farms, especially in the Cape vineyards. In flight the red wings are conspicuous.

VOICE
The Redwinged Starling makes a variety of mellow whistles 'peeeoo', 'peetu' or 'wheeoo-teeoo' etc., either while perched or flying. These notes also form the basis of a melancholy song sequence.

NESTING
The Redwinged Starling breeds October–March. It builds a substantial bowl-type nest of grasses and twigs stiffened with mud and lined with hair or plant fibres, pine needles, etc. This is placed in a hole, crevice or ledge on a cliff or building and three to five eggs are laid. These are incubated by the female for about 16 days. After hatching the nestlings are fed by both parents for about 26 days before fledging. The species often raises two broods in a season.

A male Redwinged Starling removing a faecal sac from its nest on an outhouse roof-beam.

The Redwinged Starling lays eggs of a light bluish-green colour, lightly spotted with reddish-brown. They are on average 33,5 mm in length.

IN THE GARDEN
During summertime the Redwinged Starling visits gardens where trees are in fruit, being especially attracted to grapes. At other times of the year it can be attracted to bird tables with offerings of fruit, bone-meal and mealie pap. These birds will also pick burnt meat morsels from barbecue grids.

A female Redwinged Starling showing clearly its grey head.

This species is present over much of South Africa but is absent in the north-western Cape where it is replaced by the closely related Palewinged Starling. It occurs commonly as a garden bird in Cape Town and its suburbs, Port Elizabeth, East London and Pietermaritzburg, less frequently on the Witwatersrand.

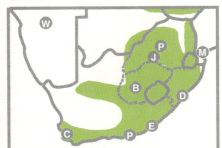

Malachite Sunbird
NATIONAL NUMBER 775
and
Black Sunbird
NATIONAL NUMBER 792

OTHER NAMES: MALACHITE SUNBIRD
Jangroentjie
Nectarinia famosa

The male Malachite Sunbird in breeding plumage is unmistakable. However, when not breeding it resembles the female though retaining a few green feathers on the wings and, sometimes, also the long tail. The yellow shoulder tufts of the male are extended when the bird is excited. The male spends much time chasing rivals or calling from the top of a bush.

VOICE
The male Malachite calls, usually from atop a bush, 'chew-chew-chew, chi-chi-chi-chiew . . . chit-chit-chit . . .' with variations in speed and sequence.

NESTING
In the winter rainfall regions the Malachite Sunbird breeds between June and December with an August peak, in the summer rainfall regions from August to March. The nest is an oval structure of dried grasses, plant fibres, rootlets and dried leaves with an entrance near the top beneath a porch of grass heads. It is suspended from a hillside bush or a branch over water. Two or three eggs are laid, the female incubating them for up to 16 days. The nestlings are fed by both parents for up to 21 days.

The creamy-white eggs of the Malachite Sunbird are heavily spotted and blotched overall with olive-brown and have an average length of 19,6 mm.

IN THE GARDEN
The Malachite regularly visits gardens of towns in the fynbos region and hills in the southern Transvaal where *Leonotis*, *Ericas* and *Proteas* are in blossom. In the Transvaal its presence as a garden species is seasonal and erractic.

A female Malachite Sunbird at its nest in a Protea bush.

The Malachite Sunbird is found widely south of the Orange River and northwards into the southern Transvaal. In many regions it migrates to higher altitudes during winter.

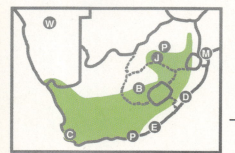

OTHER NAMES: BLACK SUNBIRD
AMETHYST SUNBIRD
Swartsuikerbekkie
Nectarinia amethystina

The male Black Sunbird is actually deep velvet-brown in colour. It has an iridescent patch of green on the head and patches of magenta or violet on the throat, shoulders and rump. The female is identified by its creamy underparts, dusky throat, large bill and the cream-yellow streak extending backwards from the gape. A restless species, it ranges widely in search of nectar-bearing flowers.

A male Black Sunbird on Protea cynaroides, *where it would extract many small insects in addition to nectar. Photo: Nico Myburgh.*

VOICE
The normal call is a sharp 'tseet', sometimes given in flight, or a prolonged series of loud 'tip, tip, tip, chip, chip, chip' notes. The male sings a low-pitched warbling song for long periods from within cover during late summer.

The eggs of the Black Sunbird are either creamy with olive-brown and blackish spots and blotches as illustrated, or pale green to pale grey with a dense overlay of olive-brown smudges. On average they are 20 mm in length.

NESTING
The breeding season is July–April in the Cape, August–March and June in Natal and throughout the summer in the Transvaal. The nest is a typical sunbird structure of dried grasses, fibres and leaves bound with spider web and with a porch topping the entrance to one side. Mostly two eggs are laid and incubated for about 15 days by the female; both parents feed the young during the 19 day nestling period.

A female Black Sunbird feeding its nestlings.

The Black Sunbird ranges over most of the Transvaal and south through Swaziland, Natal and the eastern Cape coastal belt, occurring on forest edges, in woodland, parks and gardens.

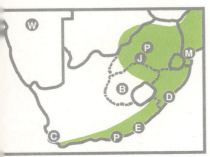

IN THE GARDEN
The Black Sunbird is a common but irregular garden visitor, feeding on *Aloes, Proteas, Ericas, Leonotis* (wild dagga), *Crotolaria* (lion's claw) and *Kniphofia* (red-hot poker), among others. It also eats spiders and hawks insects in the air. It will feed from a sugar-water feeder.

Lesser and Greater Doublecollared Sunbirds

NATIONAL NUMBERS RESPECTIVELY 783 AND 785

The doublecollared sunbirds differ only in the width of their red breast-bands plus body and bill sizes. The Lesser, found mostly at low altitudes, has a narrow red breast-band not more than 10 mm in width (often less) whereas the Greater, a bird of the hills, has a band of about 25 mm in width. Both have a liking for the nectar of plants with bell-type flowers, *Aloes, Leonotis, Erythrina, Erica,* golden shower, honeysuckle, bottlebrush, etc., in addition to insects and spiders. Like all sunbirds they dart about restlessly from plant to plant while feeding or in erratic chases. The females are dull grey-brown birds.

OTHER NAMES: LESSER D.C. SUNBIRD
Klein-rooiborssuikerbekkie
Nectarinia chalybea

OTHER NAMES: GREATER D.C. SUNBIRD
Groot-rooiborssuikerbekkie
Nectarinia afra

VOICE
Both Lesser and Greater Doublecollared Sunbirds utter a rapid jumble of high-pitched notes in bursts of several seconds. Otherwise they call 'zeep-zeep' while chasing. Recently fledged young maintain a monotonous 'zeep, zeep, zeep, zeep . . .' all day when calling for food.

A female Lesser Doublecollared Sunbird feeding on an Erica *flower. Photo: Peter Steyn.*

NESTING

The doublecollared sunbirds may breed at any time but favour October–December. In both species the nest is a pear-shaped pocket constructed of dry grass, plant fibres, dried leaves and spider webs warmly lined with plant down and feathers and having an entrance to one side near the top. In the Greater a porch always extends over the entrance, less often so in the Lesser. The nest is suspended from a branch amidst a leaf cluster, seldom more than three metres above ground. Two eggs are normally laid and incubated by the female for up to 16 days. The nestling period is 15–19 days, the chicks being fed by both parents during this time and after fledging.

A male Lesser Doublecollared Sunbird hover-feeding from an Erica. *Photo: Peter Steyn.*

This male Lesser Doublecollared Sunbird is in its eclipse, non-breeding plumage. Photo: Peter Steyn.

A male Greater Doublecollared Sunbird feeding from an Aloe *flower. Photo: Peter Steyn.*

The eggs of the Lesser Doublecollared Sunbird are basically creamy in colour with a densely mottled overlay of dull olive-brown or greyish. Their average length is 16 mm.

The eggs of the Greater Doublecollared Sunbird are elongated, buff or whitish with a marbled overlay of greyish and pale olive-brown, blotched with dark brown. They have an average length of 18,5 mm.

IN THE GARDEN

Where they occur both species will visit gardens with suitable flowering plants as mentioned in the introduction to the species. They are unlikely to visit bird tables but will be attracted to sugar-water feeders.

The Lesser Doublecollared Sunbird is found from the Orange River mouth southwards in a broad band through Namaqualand and the Karoo to about Port Elizabeth; it also extends in a narrow band north along the coast to southern Natal and inland east of the Drakensberg range to the northern Transvaal.

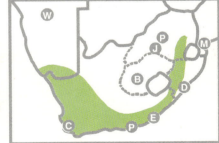

The Greater Doublecollared Sunbird is found in coastal and montane forests from Cape Town northwards to the northern Transvaal.

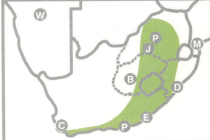

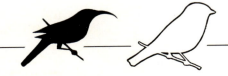

Whitebellied Sunbird

NATIONAL NUMBER 787

OTHER NAMES
Witpenssuikerbekkie
Nectarinia talatala

VOICE
The male Whitebellied Sunbird sings for long periods from a treetop during the breeding season, a shrill, much-repeated 'chu-ee, chu-ee, chu-ee-trrrr'. It also has a 'chak-chak' alarm call.

This colourful little sunbird has become a common breeding species in many towns, favouring well-wooded gardens and parks. As with most sunbirds the sexes of the Whitebellied show very distinct plumage differences. The iridescent colouring of the male's head, mantle and breast is more bluish than in most other species, and is separated from the white belly by a purple band. The small female is fairly easily recognised because of its pure white underparts, lacking in most other female sunbirds. Usually they are seen in pairs and, although partial to nectar, they feed on many small insects, and spiders, which they will often take from beneath window ledges.

A male Whitebellied Sunbird at its typically untidy nest.

NESTING
The Whitebellied Sunbird breeds at almost any time of the year but has a distinct peak during September–December. The nest is an untidy pear-shaped structure of grass, leaves and vegetable down bound with spider web and with an entrance near the top at one side covered by a small porch. It is lined with vegetable down and suspended to an outer twig of a small bush. The two eggs are incubated by the female for about 13 days. The nestling period is about 15 days during which both parents feed the young. The species probably raises two broods in a season.

The eggs of the Whitebellied Sunbird are variable, being basically creamy in colour, heavily blotched in dark brown around the broad end (left), mottled overall with pale brown (centre) or variably spotted and scrawled with dark brown and grey (right). Their average length is 16 mm.

The Whitebellied Sunbird occurs from southern Natal through the eastern half of the province, Swaziland and over most of the Transvaal except the south-east. Normally it prefers dry woodland and *Acacia* savanna.

IN THE GARDEN
Whereas the Whitebellied Sunbird may spend many weeks or even a few months in a locality it will just as suddenly disappear, these movements probably being influenced by the availability of flowering plants. Its presence in the garden is therefore sporadic although a pair will often build their nest and breed if circumstances are favourable. It will not visit a bird table but can be attracted to sugar-water in a sunbird-feeder.

Cape White-eye

NATIONAL NUMBER 796

OTHER NAMES
Kaapse Glasogie; Groenglasogie
Zosterops pallidus

The well-known white-eyes vary in colour according to locality: those from Natal are generally greener (top illustration), those from the Transvaal Highveld are more yellow (central illustration) while the western Cape birds (lower illustration) are greyer below. Between these basic colour forms a variety of intermediate forms occur. The Cape White-eye normally occurs in small flocks (larger flocks after breeding), visiting flowering trees, creepers and plants in search of nectar and small insects. Individuals explore leaves, branches and leaf-buds while reaching and hanging in a variety of attitudes before all trailing off to the next tree. The sexes are alike.

VOICE
The normal contact call within a flock while feeding is a melancholy 'phe'; during the breeding season the male sings a loud, rambling song from a treetop. It also sings a subdued warbling song from the depths of a bush.

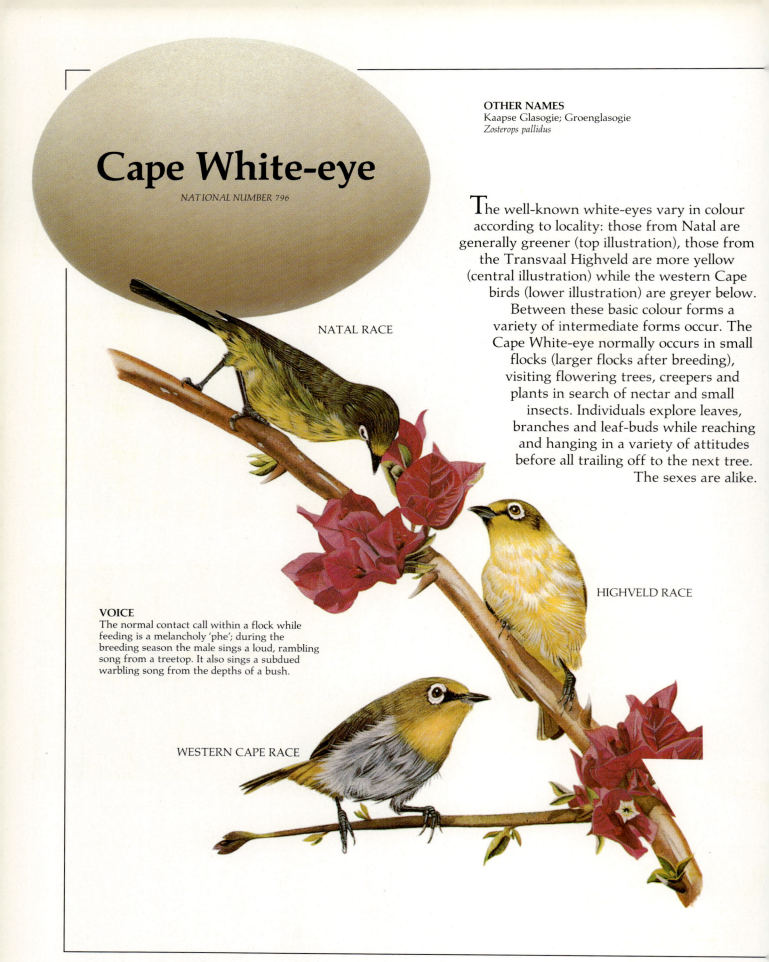

NATAL RACE

HIGHVELD RACE

WESTERN CAPE RACE

NESTING

The Cape White-eye breeds August–April with an October–November peak in the western Cape, October–January in the Transvaal and Natal. The nest, placed in a branch-fork of a leafy tree, is a small cup of fibres and tendrils covered with moss and spider web and lined with fine grass or plant down, in which two or three eggs are laid. Both sexes incubate for 11 days and feed the nestlings for 12–13 days.

The Cape White-eye lays either immaculate pale blue or white eggs with an average length of 17,3 mm.

IN THE GARDEN

This species is a common garden bird everywhere and needs no attracting. However, it comes to bird tables to eat soft fruits, especially pawpaw, apples, pears and grapes, and will also visit sugar-water feeders. It is also attracted to the seeds of the wild peach tree (*Kiggelaria africana*) in late summer as well as eating many aphids in the garden. The Cape White-eye is attracted to garden sprinklers and bird baths.

Cape White-eyes feeding their nestlings: above, the yellow Transvaal race; below, the western Cape race. Photo: Peter Steyn.

The Cape White-eye has a very sweet tooth and, in this remarkable photograph, is seen hovering like a sunbird at an Erica *flower. Photo: Peter Steyn.*

The Cape White-eye occurs throughout the country in a variety of wooded habitats.

House Sparrow and Cape Sparrow

NATIONAL NUMBERS RESPECTIVELY 801 AND 803

OTHER NAMES: HOUSE SPARROW
MOSSIE; ENGLISH SPARROW
Huismossie
Passer domesticus

VOICE
The House Sparrow makes a variety of cheeps, chirps and twittering sounds.

FEMALE

MALES

NESTING
The House Sparrow breeds through most of the year. The untidy nest of grass, wool, feathers and odd rubbish with a side entrance is placed usually under the eaves of a house or in a thatch. Four to six eggs are laid and incubated for 14 days by both sexes. The nestling period is 15 days, the chicks being fed by both parents.

The introduced House Sparrow is reliant on human habitations and is seldom far from the kitchen door. Like the Cape Sparrow it has a varied diet in addition to its more natural one of seeds and insects. While the male has a grey crown and black face and bib, the female is considerably plainer with few distinctive markings. It is smaller than the Cape Sparrow.

IN THE GARDEN
In the garden the House Sparrow becomes very tame. It does not compete with the Cape Sparrow in any way and is in fact subservient to it. However, it may take over the mud nests of striped swallows where these are built on buildings.

The eggs of the House Sparrow are basically white or bluish, well spotted and blotched with greyish-brown, and measure on average 21 mm in length.

The House Sparrow occurs throughout the country in human settlements, even in country camps and game lodges.

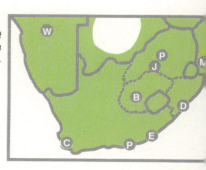

OTHER NAMES: CAPE SPARROW
CAPE MOSSIE
Gewone Mossie
Passer melanurus

The Cape Sparrow is a friendly and bold little bird which becomes very tame in towns. The diagnostic head markings, black in the male and grey in the female, make confusion with the House Sparrow unlikely. Common in parks and gardens where they thrive on household scraps, they are nevertheless basically seed-eaters.

A female Cape Sparrow feeding young at its nest.

VOICE
In addition to its normal 'chirrup' or 'chissik' call note the Cape Sparrow's song is made up of a jerky sequence of similar sounds.

NESTING
The Cape Sparrow breeds at almost any time of the year with a peak during summer. The nest, placed in a tree or bush, is a bulky, ragged bundle of dry grass, rags, bits of wool, string or plastic with an entrance at one end and warmly lined with feathers. It is used as a roost when the birds are not breeding. Three to six eggs are laid and incubated by both parents for up to 14 days. Both parents feed the nestlings until they fledge at about 15 days and for about 14 days afterwards.

IN THE GARDEN
In the garden the Cape Sparrow is a permanent resident which adorns the trees with its ragged nests. Bold and confiding, it is a regular visitor to bird tables, eating almost anything available.

The Cape Sparrow's eggs are white, greenish or bluish well spotted and blotched with grey-brown, dark brown and lilac forming a cap at the broad end. Their average length is 20 mm.

The Cape Sparrow occurs over most of the country except eastern Natal and the Transvaal Lowveld, but its distribution is often patchy within its range. Most commonly seen in urban areas and farmlands.

Spectacled and Spottedbacked Weavers

NATIONAL NUMBERS RESPECTIVELY 810 AND 811

OTHER NAMES: SPECTACLED WEAVER
Brilwewer
Ploceus ocularis

In the Spectacled Weaver the pale yellow eyes are accentuated by the black eye-stripe, the male being further distinguished by its black bib. This weaver also has a fairly slender bill in comparison to most weavers, denoting a mainly insectivorous diet. Usually solitary or in pairs, a somewhat shy species of riverine and lowland forests, dense bush and, in eastern coastal regions, parks and gardens. There is no seasonal plumage change in either sex.

NESTING
The Spectacled Weaver breeds mainly October–January. The solitary nest with an entrance spout 25–30 cm long is suspended from a branch, palm frond or papyrus stem, often over water. Two or three eggs are laid, both sexes sharing the 13–14 day incubation and feeding the chicks during the ensuing 18 day nestling period.

VOICE
The normal call, and one that usually reveals its presence, is a descending, high-pitched 'tee-tee-tee-tee-tee-tee-tee-tee'. It also makes a throaty chattering and calls 'tseet, tseet'.

The eggs of the Spectacled Weaver are variable as illustrated: either pinkish-white, spotted and speckled with reddish-brown and grey (left), or greenish, spotted and blotched with grey-brown forming a cap at the broad end (centre) or white sparingly speckled with grey-brown. Their average length is 22 mm.

IN THE GARDEN
The Spectacled Weaver is most common in Durban and adjacent coastal districts where it enters gardens and may breed. While being mainly insectivorous and frugivorous it is also partially granivorous. At the bird table it can be attracted by bone-meal, fruit or bird seed and may well build its nest over a garden pond or swimming pool.

The Spectacled Weaver occurs along the coastal belt from about Port Elizabeth to Zululand, over much of Natal, Swaziland and the eastern and north-eastern Transvaal.

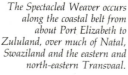

OTHER NAMES: SPOTTEDBACKED WEAVER
Bontrugwewer
Ploceus cucullatus

The Spottedbacked Weaver resembles the Masked Weaver (page 116) but the male differs in that the black mask does not extend onto the forehead while the upperparts are black, heavily spotted yellow. The female can be told from the female Masked by larger, sharper bill plus yellow breast and white belly. In the non-breeding season the male resembles the female.

A male Spottedbacked Weaver building a nest: note how the leaves of the tree have been incorporated into the roof.

VOICE
The Spottedbacked makes a similar husky, swizzling sound to that of the Masked Weaver 'shrrrrr zzzzzrrrr zezezezeze . . .', especially when displaying beneath the nest with fluttering wings.

NESTING
This species breeds colonially mainly August–February. The male has one or two mates and builds several nests during the season, these being similar to those of the Masked Weaver but more ovoid in shape, usually with a short entrance spout and with leaves woven into the roof. The nests, often many dozens in a colony, are suspended from the ends of drooping branches on trees, bushes or between reed stems. The female lines the nest with grass heads, strips the supporting branch of leaves and lays two or three eggs which she incubates for 12 days. The nestling period lasts up to 21 days during which the male helps the female feed the chicks.

In the Spottedbacked Weaver the eggs are highly variable as shown: either plain blue-green (left), blue-green well spotted grey-brown (left centre), pinkish well spotted in shades of brown (centre), plain white (right centre), or pink mottled overall with brown. The average length is 23,5 mm.

IN THE GARDEN
The Spottedbacked Weaver enters parks and gardens usually near water, and will breed in gardens with a water feature. It can be attracted to bird tables with a variety of food scraps including bone-meal, mealie pap and seeds.

The Spottedbacked Weaver is found in the coastal belt from about Port Elizabeth to northern Natal, in Swaziland and over much of the Transvaal, where its presence is patchy.

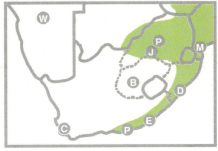

Cape Weaver
NATIONAL NUMBER 813

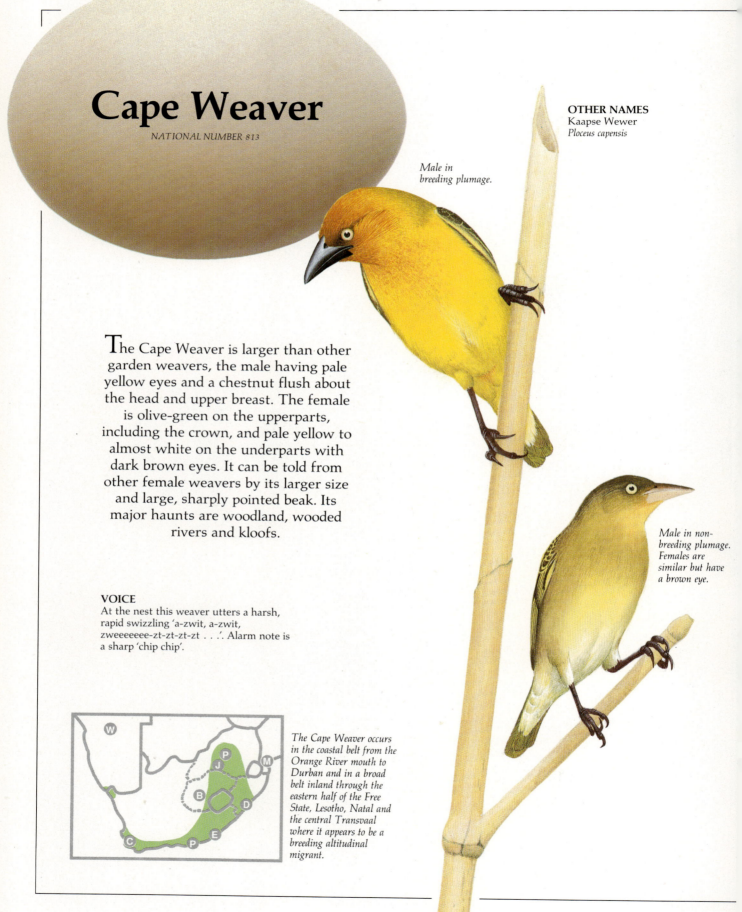

Male in breeding plumage.

OTHER NAMES
Kaapse Wewer
Ploceus capensis

Male in non-breeding plumage. Females are similar but have a brown eye.

The Cape Weaver is larger than other garden weavers, the male having pale yellow eyes and a chestnut flush about the head and upper breast. The female is olive-green on the upperparts, including the crown, and pale yellow to almost white on the underparts with dark brown eyes. It can be told from other female weavers by its larger size and large, sharply pointed beak. Its major haunts are woodland, wooded rivers and kloofs.

VOICE
At the nest this weaver utters a harsh, rapid swizzling 'a-zwit, a-zwit, zweeeeeee-zt-zt-zt-zt . . .'. Alarm note is a sharp 'chip chip'.

The Cape Weaver occurs in the coastal belt from the Orange River mouth to Durban and in a broad belt inland through the eastern half of the Free State, Lesotho, Natal and the central Transvaal where it appears to be a breeding altitudinal migrant.

This male Cape Weaver is building its nest between two papyrus stems; it will complete the shell and the female will add a lining of plant down. Photo: Peter Steyn.

A male Cape Weaver in non-breeding plumage. Note its pale yellow eye.

NESTING

The Cape Weaver breeds July–October in the Cape, mainly November–January in Natal and mainly September–October in the Transvaal where its nesting cycle is normally completed well before that of other weavers. The male is polygamous. Nests are built in small colonies of five to ten attached to reeds, hanging branches on bushes over water or in exotic trees. They are kidney-shaped orbs with an entrance beneath and woven with broad strips of grass or reed, and are larger than those of the Masked Weaver. Two or three eggs are laid and incubated by the female for 14 days; the male assists the female in feeding the chicks for the 17 day nestling period.

The kidney-shaped nests of the Cape Weaver.

The eggs of the Cape Weaver are greenish-blue and somewhat elongated, measuring on average 25 mm in length.

IN THE GARDEN

In coastal regions the Cape Weaver is regularly seen in gardens, but elsewhere it is less frequent and seasonal. It will come readily to a bird table stocked with seeds, bone-meal, bread or mealie pap, at which time its larger size when compared to other weavers and sparrows can be appreciated. It also takes nectar from certain flowers in season, its face becoming covered in pollen as a result.

Masked Weaver

NATIONAL NUMBER 814

OTHER NAMES
Swartkeelgeelvink
Ploceus velatus

The breeding male can be confused with the male Spottedbacked Weaver (page 113) but note that in the Masked Weaver the black mask extends across the forehead; also it lacks the spotted back of the other species. A very common garden bird in many towns, conspicuous in summer as the males build their many nests, stripping leaves off trees as they do so to display more prominently to the females. A gregarious species at all times.

NESTING
The main breeding period is September–March but in many localities the male starts building nests as early as May–June and continues until April. Being a polygamous, colonial nester the male builds many nests in a season, often festooning the trees with them. The nest is of a hanging ball-type with an entrance below and built of fresh green grass which, however, soon dries. When the nest is completed the male hangs below it, calling with flapping wings to attract a female who, if interested, will line the nest. If the female rejects the nest, the male destroys it. Four or five eggs are laid and incubated by the female. There are no records of the incubation or nestling times.

VOICE
The male makes a harsh swizzling sound 'zzzzrrrr-zik-zik-zik . . .' during much of the year plus an occasional sharp 'zik'.

Masked Weavers at the bird table.

A male Masked Weaver assuming breeding plumage.

A male Masked Weaver in non-breeding plumage.

A female Masked Weaver non-breeding plumage.

IN THE GARDEN
The Masked Weaver is a very common garden bird in most towns at all times of the year. Basically a granivorous and frugivorous species, it will nevertheless eat almost anything put on the bird table.

The eggs of the Masked Weaver are highly variable, being either pink with an overall mottling of red-brown (left), pale blue-green (left centre), pale buff well spotted in shades of brown (centre), blue-green mottled and spotted overall in brown (right centre) or pale olive-green well spotted and blotched with dark brown (right). Also occasionally pure white. The average length is 20 mm.

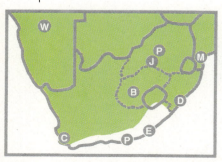

The Masked Weaver is very common throughout most of the country, except in the eastern Cape coastal region, and is found in a wide range of habitats.

A male Masked Weaver building a nest. Once the basic shell is completed it will either be lined by a female or destroyed by the male. A male can complete a nest in less than six hours.

Red Bishop

NATIONAL NUMBER 824

OTHER NAMES
Rooivink
Euplectes orix

The male Red Bishop fluffs its plumage while perched conspicuously to advertise its breeding territory to other males.

A male with its breeding plumage sleeked.

Female.

During the summer the male Red Bishop is quite unmistakable as it perches on a reed stem puffing out its scarlet plumage in territorial display. At this time it is found in reedbeds where it breeds, but in the non-breeding season it assumes drab plumage like the female and forms flocks, feeding in grasslands, vleis and farmlands and roosting in reeds at night. It frequently forages in gardens near dams and rivers.

A male Red Bishop in the process of changing from its drab winter plumage to its breeding colours. This process takes about ten days.

VOICE
When displaying in the breeding season the male utters a harsh 'zik zik zik . . .' and a wheezy 'zay zay zay zay zay . . .'.

NESTING
Breeding occurs according to regional rainfall patterns; as early as July in the south-western Cape, September–March in Natal and the Transvaal. It breeds in large colonies in reedbeds, occasionally in smaller colonies in bushes near water reservoirs and other man-made water impoundments. The male, which usually has several mates, builds a number of thin-walled, oval nests with a canopied entrance to one side near the top; a female may assist in nest-building. The nests are placed between reed stems over water, rarely between vertical branches of a bush. The female lines the nest with plant down or grass heads and lays three eggs. She alone incubates for up to 14 days and cares for the chicks during the 12–16 day nestling period.

The eggs of the Red Bishop are immaculate pale blue and measure on average 19–20 mm in length.

A female Red Bishop assisting with nest-building, a task normally left to the male.

IN THE GARDEN
The Red Bishop is attracted to bird tables with seeds or mealie pap, or can be attracted to seed cast on the ground. It will build nests at garden ponds where reeds or papyrus grows although these breeding attempts are seldom successful.

The Red Bishop occurs everywhere except in the extreme northen Cape and parts of the Transvaal, invariably near vleis, marshes, dams and rivers.

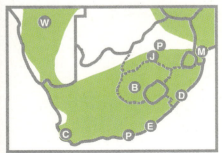

A female Red Bishop at the nest with a faecal sac taken from a nestling. During the non-breeding season the male assumes a similar plumage to that of the female.

Bronze Mannikin

NATIONAL NUMBER 857

OTHER NAMES
FRET
Gewone Fret
Spermestes cucullatus

These brownish, miniature sparrow-like birds usually occur in flocks of up to 30. Adults have black heads, a bronze-green patch on the shoulder and white underparts with barred flanks, while juveniles are much duller and lack the black head and barred flanks. Between the two extremes is the sub-adult stage as illustrated in the two lower birds. Flocks spend much time feeding in compact groups on the ground or hanging on grass heads. If disturbed they fly up suddenly into the nearest bush, later dropping back to the feeding place in ones and twos. When roosting, several birds huddle together, either in a nest or some other sheltered spot such as in a cluster of palm fronds.

IMMATURES

This species is found in a narrow coastal strip from Port Elizabeth to Natal, and throughout Natal, Swaziland, the north-eastern Free State and all but the western Transvaal. It frequents thickets, wooded savanna, old cultivations and gardens.

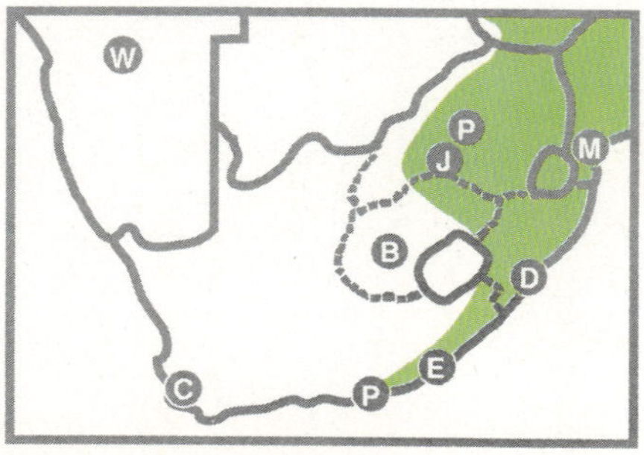

VOICE
Flocks make wheezy little 'chit chit chit' or 'chuk chuk chuk' sounds plus a rapid 'tsree tsree tsree' call.

NESTING
Breeding takes place during the summer at which time flocks break up into pairs or small family groups. The nest is a large, untidy dome of fine dried grasses with a side entrance, and placed conspicuously in a bush or creeper. Four to six eggs are laid and incubated for about 15 days by both sexes. Both sexes also feed the chicks during the 17–23 day nestling period.

A Bronze Mannikin in full adult plumage. Photo: Nico Myburgh.

The nest of the Bronze Mannikin is frequently placed among palm fronds.

The Bronze Mannikin lays immaculate white eggs measuring on average 14 mm in length.

IN THE GARDEN
The Bronze Mannikin is a common garden species in Natal and occasionally in parts of the Reef. It feeds on small grass seeds, insects and plant material, and can be attracted to bird tables with bird seed, mealie pap and table scraps. It is also attracted to bird-baths.

A flock of Bronze Mannikins settling at a temporary roost. Photo: Peter Ginn.

Pintailed Whydah

NATIONAL NUMBER 860

OTHER NAMES
KING OF SIX
Koningrooibekkie; Koningweduweetjie
Vidua macroura

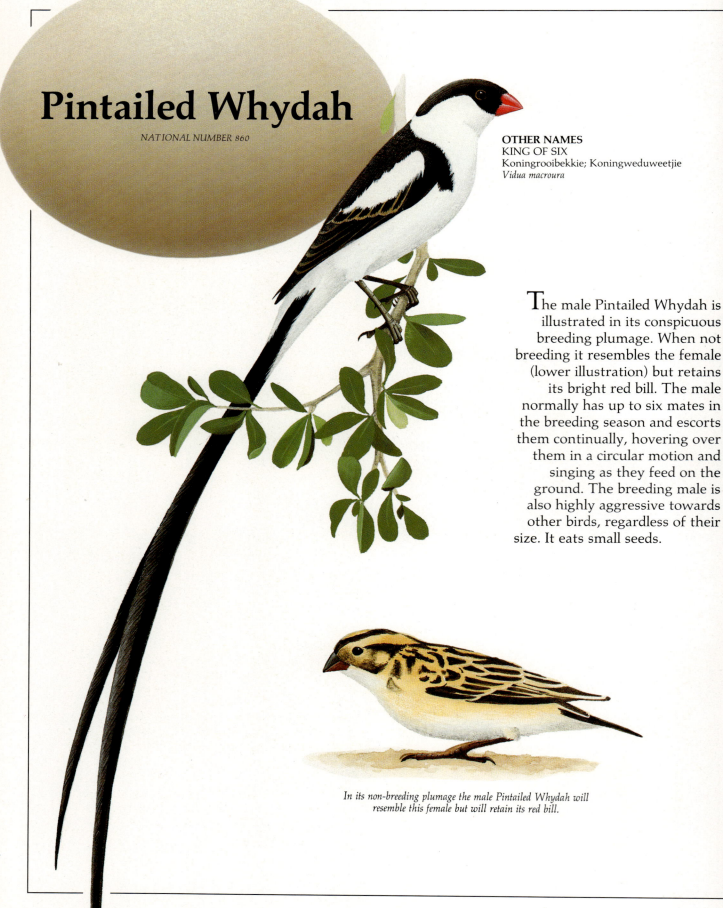

The male Pintailed Whydah is illustrated in its conspicuous breeding plumage. When not breeding it resembles the female (lower illustration) but retains its bright red bill. The male normally has up to six mates in the breeding season and escorts them continually, hovering over them in a circular motion and singing as they feed on the ground. The breeding male is also highly aggressive towards other birds, regardless of their size. It eats small seeds.

In its non-breeding plumage the male Pintailed Whydah will resemble this female but will retain its red bill.

VOICE
The song, sung mostly during courtship, is a high-pitched, whispy 'peetzy peetzy peetzy peetzy . . .' as the male hovers over the female. It also calls 'sip, sip' in flight.

NESTING
This common and widespread little bird is a brood parasite, laying its eggs in the nests of other small birds, mostly the Common Waxbill, Bronze Mannikin and Orangebreasted Waxbill. This occurs mainly during the period November–March. The young whydahs are reared together with the young of the host and remain together for some time after fledging.

IN THE GARDEN
The Pintailed Whydah is a common garden species in many regions where it is usually attracted to seed on the bird table. However, the male can become a nuisance, acting aggressively towards other small birds attempting to feed. It will drive off anything up to the size of a dove, reserving the table strictly for its own females. In such a case seeds should not be put on the bird table but scattered elsewhere on the ground or not offered at all, since other seed-eaters will take bread or mealie pap, whereas the whydahs will not.

A female Pintailed Whydah is about to enter the ground nest of a Common Waxbill in order to deposit her own eggs.

The unsuspecting Common Waxbill returning to its parasitised nest.

The Pintailed Whydah is found throughout the country in a wide range of habitats.

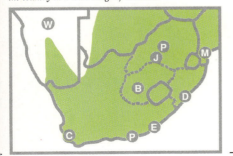

Eggs taken from the nest of an Orangebreasted Waxbill, the small ones being those of the host and the larger ones, measuring 11 mm in length, those of a Pintailed Whydah.

Cape Canary and Yelloweyed Canary

NATIONAL NUMBERS RESPECTIVELY 872 AND 869

OTHER NAMES: CAPE CANARY
Kaapse Kanarie
Serinus canicollis

OTHER NAMES: YELLOWEYED CANARY
Geeloogkanarie
Serinus mozambicus

VOICE OF THE CAPE CANARY
The Cape Canary has a wild, prolonged song during the breeding season. At other times it sings a short song at brief intervals 'peety-weety-weety-weety-sweeeee', always descending in pitch at the end.

Cape Canaries occur as garden birds in the Cape Town region and in Pietermaritzburg. The sexes are closely similar, the blue-grey colouring of the nape and mantle being diagnostic. Usually seen in flocks when not breeding, either singing in trees or feeding on seeding grasses.

The Cape Canary is distributed from the south-western Cape through the coastal belt to northern Natal and inland through the eastern half of the Free State and southern Transvaal northwards along the Drakensberg escarpment.

NESTING (CAPE CANARY)
This canary breeds mainly September–October in the south-western Cape, July–December in the eastern Cape and August–December in Natal and the Transvaal. The female builds a compact cup-shaped nest of grass and tendrils warmly lined with plant down and placed in the fork of a horizontal tree branch. Three or four eggs are laid, the female incubating them for 12–14 days. Both parents feed the chicks during the 15–18 day nestling period.

The Yelloweyed Canary (it has brown eyes!) is common in coastal towns from Port Elizabeth northwards. This canary usually occurs in flocks or small groups which feed on the ground on the seeds of grasses and weeds. It enjoys a wide range of habitats at both low and higher altitudes with a preference for bushveld.

VOICE OF THE YELLOWEYED CANARY
The normal call is 'tseeu' but it also has a cheery, high-pitched song given in short outbursts.

NESTING (YELLOWEYED CANARY)
This canary breeds September–April. Both sexes build the nest, a deep, compact cup of grasses, rootlets, tendrils and seed heads bound together and to the branch with spider webs. The nest is placed in the fork of a horizontal branch in a bush or tree. Three to four eggs are laid and incubated by the female for 13–14 days. The nestling period is 16–24 days during which both parents feed the chicks.

A male Cape Canary at its nest amidst growing grapes in the Cape. The nestlings of this species are fed by the male on a regurgitated mash of partially digested seeds. The male removes their droppings up to the eighth day and thereafter they are deposited on the edge of the nest and are not removed.

The eggs of both canaries are similar, being pinkish-white lightly spotted with reddish-brown. That of the Yelloweyed Canary is shown on the left and has an average length of 16,5 mm while the egg of the Cape Canary is shown on the right, and has an average length of 17,3 mm.

CANARIES IN THE GARDEN
The Cape Canary is not easily attracted by bird seed or mealie pap on the bird table but does frequent bird-baths, whereas the Yelloweyed Canary readily visits bird tables, feeding on bird seed, mealie pap and scraps, and will also use bird-baths. It also feeds on grass heads on overgrown urban road verges.

A Cape Canary bathing in a garden pond. Bathing is an important part of plumage maintenance in most birds. Photo: Peter Steyn.

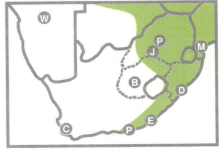

The Yelloweyed Canary ranges through the coastal regions from about Port Elizabeth to Durban and over most of Natal, Swaziland, the northern Free State and all but the western Transvaal, occurring almost anywhere within this range.

Appendix

Some indigenous plants, shrubs and trees attractive to birds

SCIENTIFIC NAME	POPULAR NAMES	TYPE	FOOD
Acacia species	Kaffir-thorn; monkey-thorn; camel-thorn; sweet-thorn; knob-thorn; paperbark-thorn; etc.	trees	flowers, nectar and seeds
Acokanthera oppositifolia	Hottentot's poison bush	shrub	fruit
Aloe species	Aloe	succulent plants	nectar
Annona senegalensis		tree	fruit
Bequaertiodendron magalismontanum	Stamvrug	shrub	fruit
Berchemia zeyheri	Red-ivory; rooihout	tree	fruit
Boscia albitrunca	Shepherd's tree; witgat	tree	fruit
Boscia oleoides	Witgat; shepherd's tree	tree	fruit
Bridelia species	Mitzeerie	tree	fruit
Carissa bispinosa	Num-num	shrub	fruit
Celtis africana	White stinkwood	tree	fruit
Crotalaria capensis	Cape rattlepod	shrub	nectar
Diospyros species	Blue-bush; monkey plum; Transvaal ebony; black-bark, etc.	trees	fruit
Diplorhynchus condylocarpon		tree	fruit
Dovyalis caffra	Kei-apple; Dingaan's apricot	shrub or tree	fruit
Ehretia rigida	Cape lilac	shrub	fruit
Ekebergia capensis	Dog plum; essenhout	tree	fruit
Erica species	Bridal heath; Knysna heath; green heath; etc.	shrubs	nectar
Erythrina species	Kaffirboom; luckybean trees	trees	nectar and seeds
Euclea species	Gwarri trees	trees and shrubs	fruit
Eugenia species		trees	fruit
Euphorbia ingens	Naboom, candelabra tree	tree-succulent	fruit
Fagara species	Knobwood	trees and shrubs	fruit
Ficus species	Wild figs	trees	fruit
Flacourtia species		trees and shrubs	fruit
Garcinia species	Mangosteen	trees	fruit
Gardenia species	Gardenia	shrubs	flowers, nectar and fruit
Greyia sutherlandii	Natal bottlebrush	tree	nectar
Halleria lucida	Notsung; tree fuchsia	shrub or tree	nectar and fruit
Harpephyllum caffrum	Kaffir plum	tree	fruit
Heeria argentea	Resin-bush	shrub	fruit
Kigelia africana	Sausage tree	tree	nectar
Kiggelaria africana	Wild peach; porkwood	shurb or tree	fruit
Kniphofia species	Red-hot pokers	plants	nectar
Lannea species	Bakhout; dikbas; bastermaroela	trees	fruit
Leonotis leonurus	Wild dagga	plant	nectar
Leucosidea sericea	Ouhout	shrub or small tree	fruit

Maytenus species	Pendoring	shrubs	fruit
Mimusops species	Milkwoods	trees	fruit
Ochna species	Ochna; lekkerbreek	trees and shrubs	fruit
Ocotea bullata	Black stinkwood; Cape laurel; Cape olive	tree	fruit
Olea species	Wild olive; black ironwood; etc.	trees	fruit
Olinia species	Hard pear; rooibessie	trees	fruit
Oncoba spinosa	Snuffbox tree	shrub	fruit
Pappea capensis	Wild plum	shrub or tree	fruit
Parinari curatellifolia	Mobola plum; hissing tree; sandapple; cork tree	tree	fruit
Pavetta species	Bride's bushes	trees	fruit
Phoenix reclinata	Wild date palm	tree	fruit
Phygelius species	Cape fuchsia	shrubs	nectar
Pittosporum viridiflorum	Cheesewood	tree	fruit
Podocarpus elongatus		tree	fruit
Protea species	Sugar bush; suikerbossie; protea	small trees and shrubs	nectar
Rapanea melanophloeos		tree	fruit
Rhamnus prinoides	Blinkblaar	shrub	fruit
Rhus lancea	Karee; bastard willow	small tree	fruit
Rhus pyroides	Common taaibos; fire-thorn	small tree	fruit
Rothmannia species	Aapsekos; September bells; wild gardenia; etc.	trees	flowers, nectar and fruit
Schotia afra and related species	Boerboon; boer-bean	shrubs and trees	nectar and seed
Sclerocarya caffra	Marula	tree	fruit
Scolopia species	Red pear; thorn pear; etc.	trees	fruit
Spirostachys africana	Tamboti; sandalwood; jumping-bean tree	tree	fruit
Strelitzia nicolai	Blue and white strelitzia; wild banana	palm-like tree	fruit-substance
Syzygium species	Water berry; water pear; etc.	trees	fruit
Tecomaria capensis	Cape honeysuckle	creeper	nectar
Trema orientalis	Trema	tree	fruit
Vangueria infausta	Wild medlar	tree or shrub	fruit
Watsonia species	Watsonia	plants	nectar
Xanthocercis zambesiaca	Nyala tree	tree	fruit
Ximenia species	Sour plum	shrubs and trees	fruit

References

Jensen, R.A.C. (1979) 'The brood parasites' In *Birdlife in Southern Africa* (Newman, K.B. (Ed.)) pp. 175-90. Macmillan South Africa, Johannesburg.

Maclean, G.L. (1985) *Roberts' Birds of Southern Africa*. The Trustees of the John Voelcker Bird Book Fund, Cape Town.

Winterbottom, J.M. (1971) *Priest's Eggs of Southern African Birds*. Winchester Press, Johannesburg.